Cherry Tree Dares:
Essays on Childhood

Cherry Tree Dares:
Essays on Childhood

by Ilene W. Devlin

Cherry Tree Dares:
Essays on Childhood

© 2020 Ilene Whitworth Devlin

ORDERING INFORMATION: Additional copies may be obtained from the author: ilenewd@icloud.com or 210-854-6593.

ISBN – 978-1-7357340-1-9

All photographs (cover and interior) © Ilene Whitworth Devlin, 2020. Front cover: Cutler-Donahue Bridge in the Winterset City Park, Winterset, Iowa. Back cover and interior page: Madison County Courthouse, Winterset, Iowa.

DEDICATION

To all those from small towns
or who wish they were.

TABLE OF CONTENTS

PREFACE

Midwesterners in small towns have often been the brunt of jokes by city folks. I hope, however, that my essays shed literary light on what made small town life special during the mid-1950s and early 1960s. This book covers highlights of my life from ages four and a half through nearly twelve years old.

Granted, people in the small town where I grew up did tend to be a bit isolationist in their worldview. Winterset young men, however, proudly served abroad in the military. The Korean conflict raged early in the period, and the Vietnam conflict began in earnest. Others had served in World Wars I and II and still gathered at the local American Legion and VFW halls.

Our small-town residents knew the outside world existed, but it rarely impacted their daily lives. Why worry about something they could not control? Community life was of more interest to them in rearing their families and setting good examples for their grandchildren.

Isolation also had its advantages. People in Winterset truly had a community spirit. A town small enough so everyone knew everyone else's personal business could be considered a detriment. The lack of privacy was an advantage, however, when people had an emergency. Within a few hours, when people needed help, their friends heard the news and called to offer assistance.

Isolation also meant children had to use their imaginations for entertainment. In the pre-computer, pre-Internet, pre-video games era, we children played outdoors more than children do now. We knew the other neighborhood children and used their individual talents in our play whenever possible.

Ordinary objects become cherished centers of play activity. The value of a hard maple tree included shade, fall leaves in which to play, and shapes scary enough to frighten even the bravest child on Halloween nights. A hammer and a saw were invitations to make childhood construction projects of unlimited imagination.

The streets of a 1950s and 1960s small town were also safer than most neighborhoods today. People had no need to lock their doors in my neighborhood unless they left town for several days. All the neighbors kept watch on each other's property, as well as on all the neighborhood children. With such a low crime rate, however, they mainly watched for curiosity's sake, not because of the threat of criminal activity.

My former neighbors can rest assured that the names mentioned herein have been changed. Those from the old neighborhood who still live in Winterset might guess who I have described.

I have tried to write only in praise and fond memory about several people who are deceased. In some cases, I have used their real names. I hope they will be honored by the incidents I have related.

Small-town life forever impresses its memories upon those who have lived there. Winterset is still a small town in many ways. I hope it continues to be proud of this fact. I am proud to call it home, for while I may live elsewhere, I am *from* Winterset.

ACKNOWLEDGEMENTS

To Jan Kilby, whose professional advice and devoted friendship encouraged me to compose this book. Thanks for teaching me to write more professionally and for having faith in my writing attempts.

To my editor, Lillie Ammann, for her expert guidance in refining my writing.

To Rita Mayer, who offered years of support and encouragement, I am grateful you urged me to expand my horizons.

To my parents and sister, who endured my wanderlust all these years, I thank you for your patience.

To all my teachers, especially in English, who fueled my imagination through the world of books with their unlimited travel through time and space, I thank you for the journey.

WINTERSET, IOWA

Madison County Courthouse
(Photo by Ilene W. Devlin)

SETTING OF THE STORIES: MY HOMETOWN

Everyone's life journey begins somewhere. Mine began in the heart of Iowa, just thirty-five miles southwest of Des Moines, the capital. Winterset, Iowa, is one of the hubs of the state's farming belt. The area is the last semi-flat land before the rolling hills of southern Iowa begin.

In 1849, so the story goes, the founding fathers reportedly held a meeting to decide on the town's name. The men happened to convene on one incredibly hot July day. (No women were recorded in attendance at that auspicious event.) As legend goes, one leading citizen suggested the name Summerset. "It's freezing in the winters here. Call it *Winterset*," someone said sarcastically. Thus, the town's name refers to its cold winter climate, not to the nature of its citizens.

From its founding, Winterset's citizens have always been sensible, stalwart, and stoic. Known for being nice people in a nice town, they liked it that way. Nothing much exciting ever happened in Winterset, which the adult inhabitants considered desirable. The younger folks had different opinions.

With a steady population of just under 3,500 in the 1950s, Winterset never grew any larger during my childhood. Newborns or those moving in about equally replaced those who died or moved away. Life formed a continuum in Winterset when I arrived in town in mid-1957.

Madison County, of which Winterset is the county seat, proudly possessed seven of the eleven covered bridges left in Iowa. Several opinions detail why the bridges were covered. One thought was to keep ice and snow off the bridge surfaces in winter. That prevented the horses from slipping and either breaking their legs or sliding with their buggies and passengers into creeks. Another point of view was covering the bridges preserved the wooden structure longer, thus lessening replacement costs by extending the lifespan of the bridges.

The central point in Winterset is the town square. In the center of the square sits the Madison County Courthouse. Completed in 1876 and built of native white limestone, the courthouse is over five stories tall from the ground to the top of its dome. The building is shaped like a Greek Cross, with the arms extending precisely toward the north, south, east, and west. Each courthouse door opens onto a different side of the town square. Thus, I always knew my directions when I exited the courthouse.

Since it is the county seat, Winterset is considered the most important town for miles around. Folks "went to town" to Winterset to conduct their legal business, which most farmers in the area avoided whenever possible. Like their independent ancestors for generations before them, they had little use for governmental rules and regulations.

Local government officials performed well, and city government ran efficiently. Most folks, however, couldn't figure out why anyone would want to be elected to public office.

The locals went to the courthouse to buy license plates or to renew their driver's licenses. Folks fumed if they missed their birthday deadline for renewal, which required them to retake the driving test. As the rural inhabitants saw it, a guy did not have much need for some piece of paper telling him he knew how to drive. A man drove a tractor at twenty miles an hour or less most of the time. He drove the family pickup not much faster at other times so he could enjoy the beauty of the countryside.

The only rules easily tolerated were those regarding the recording of land ownership. In that mainly farming district, land ownership meant social standing in the community. Proper land deeds were essential for settling boundary disputes, the few times they ever arose.

A young man also felt great pride in recording his first purchase of farmland. Land ownership showed he was responsible enough to marry and support a family.

Most of all, farming meant the continuation of a way of life local folks valued. Farming success ensured the continued existence of the basically one-industry town.

Farming was the heart of the economy for Winterset. Many of my school friends were farm children. Most of the people I saw in church every Sunday were farm families. To a large extent, the rest of the town existed to support the farming industry.

Facing the courthouse on the four sides of the square were the merchants. Winterset boasted two five-and-dime stores, two pharmacies, men's and women's clothing stores, and a J.C. Penney franchise. Other businesses provided cloth for homemade clothes, heating equipment, food, and insurance coverage for crops and homes.

The south side held a number of companies. The

Thompson store at the southeast corner carried furnaces and small heaters, as well as delivered fuel oil and coal to homes. Ben Franklin Variety Store and Harrisons carried items from office supplies to candy, housewares, and miscellaneous goods. Harrisons had a basement where I bought my mother baking dishes or Christmas ornaments during that season. Breedings Hardware stocked hardware and some household goods such as kitchen cookware. Chas. A. Graves & Co. clothing store provided quality clothing.

Two banks, Union State on the southwest and Farmers and Merchants on the northwest corners of the square, served local residents. Their services included home mortgages, loans for seed for next year's crop, or money for a farmer's survival when a hailstorm de-stroyed that summer's crop.

On the west side resided Jackson Pharmacy, Trask Jewelry, and Montross Pharmacy. Jackson's filled prescriptions and offered medical supplies like canes and wheelchairs. Many wedding rings had been purchased at Trask's over the years. Opened in 1921, Montross Pharmacy filled prescriptions, carried medical supplies, and featured a soda fountain and sandwich counter.

The north side held more establishments. Central was the Northside Café, located in an 1876 historic building. Over the counter was a revolving ad clock, which flipped local business advertising cards to an-other offering every few minutes. Barstools lined the counter, and wooden booths provided more seating for patrons.

Other northside businesses included the pool hall and the state-owned liquor store. Folks figured that if their children were never exposed to the pool hall, they would never frequent it later in life. Many people in the church-centered town of Winterset would never have admitted publicly to enjoying an alcoholic drink.

The east side also had more businesses. The Western Auto store sat centrally located. Along with Breedings, the store provided for the hardware needs of citizens. The alley on the north side of the Western Auto had an enclosed stairway that led to the second floor. The Ma-sons and Eastern Star fraternal groups held their meet-ings there with a wonderful view of the courthouse grounds.

Also, near the northeast corner, the Iowa Theater provided one movie screen for film lovers. Flashing white lights covered the exterior marquee, drawing attention to the current film title. Inside, the aroma of popcorn filled the air, making my mouth water before I ever found my seat. The ground floor had an aisle down the middle and red velvet-covered seats on each side. Occasionally, the theater owner opened the bal-cony when additional seating was needed during a popular movie. Most teenagers headed for the upper seats when romance more than the movie piqued their interests.

I fell in love with movies at the Iowa Theater. While I would always love Winterset, I learned about the larger world while traveling through time and space at the movies.

Thus, Winterset was the hub of the county, and the courthouse served as the hub of Winterset. Seasons passed without much change in the local social struc-ture. A sense of regularity eased the spirit and freed the mind to notice other aspects of life.

A HOME FOR MY HEART

Home for me will forever be the house built in 1900 at 521 North Second Street. From the moment my four-and-a-half-year-old eyes saw the old frame house, my heart knew I was home.

The rental house dominated the large corner lot at North Second Street and Buchanan Street one block north of North Ward Elementary School. That August day in 1957, the soft grass swayed in the gentle morning breeze. Three hard maple trees shaded the street's parking area along the west side. In the backyard, two cedar trees were joined by a large board from which suspended a small rope swing. A good-sized expanse of lawn extended beyond to the east neighbor's driveway.

"Wow, what a pretty tree!" I exclaimed.

The enormous fir tree in the northside yard mesmerized me. Taller than the two-and-a-half-story house, its lower branches spread almost as wide as the house. Fallen needles carpeted the ground below, adding their aroma to the soft breeze. The wind through the branches made a low whistling sound, a sound that brought peace to any soul, no matter how troubled. When I first saw the fir tree, I could only stand in awe and absorb its presence.

When I finally returned to reality, I turned my attention to the house itself. A deep covered porch extended over half the house width on the west and south sides. The open porch had plenty of space for children to play on rainy days. On the street side, one set of porch steps led to the upstairs apartment, and another set of steps on the south connected to the door allowing us to enter the ground floor.

Today was moving day. My family was renting the ground floor and basement of the house. Upstairs, I was told, lived a couple, and we girls, my sister Kay and I, were instructed not to use the west door for that was their entrance.

I eased myself through the proper door, finding myself in the living room. The room was a medium-sized square with two tall windows facing south. The morning light flooded through the glass and shone on the polished wood floors. With its nine-foot-high ceiling, the room seemed huge to a small girl.

Across the living room, a swinging door in the east wall led to the kitchen, painted a pale yellow. A long Formica-covered counter and white porcelain sink filled half of the south side. The sink was set low, but the faucets were placed so high that I could barely reach them. Above the sink, the wallpaper had a yellow background with drawings of small kitchen tools, including rolling pins, coffee grinders, and wire whisks. Left of the sink was the back door, leading to a screened back porch. I could see beyond to the neighbor's backyard. The morning sun shone through one east window.

Opposite the back door was the door to the basement. I had always been leery of basements, with their musty smells and spiders. I decided to save exploring the basement for later. The stove and refrigerator were placed beside the basement door.

The door to the only bathroom was set in the northwest corner of the kitchen. I took due note of the bathroom's location. Two rooms children always remember are the kitchen and the bathroom. The first is for sustenance and the other for comfort, both of which are critical to childre's well-being.

The kitchen held something I had never before seen. Along the west side, a set of upper glass-fronted cabinets and lower drawers extended from floor to ceiling. Under the cabinets, I could see a rolled-up partition and directly into the living room. A person could cook in the kitchen and push the serving dishes across the flat counter to be carried into the living room. Or the partition could be lowered to hide the cooking area. What a marvelous invention.

The roomy bathroom had a light gray linoleum floor. Along the east wall was an old-fashioned, white enamel-coated, cast-iron bathtub, raised off the floor on four claw feet. Some former resident had hand painted fish on the light blue wallpaper, so I felt like I was inside an aquarium. A small window looked out onto the wonderful fir tree. The sink was installed on the south wall, while the toilet sat under the window.

My parents' bedroom was accessible from a second door in the bathroom on the west wall. I discovered a surprise when I walked into their room. Two floor-to-ceiling sliding doors separated the master bedroom from the living room.

The richly polished medium-brown wood of the doors reflected my small shadow as I gazed at them. I had never seen doors that large in any house. Yet they slid aside with little effort when pulled apart by my small arms. When fully opened, the doors disappeared into recesses in the walls.

Next was the northwest bedroom I was to share with almost one-year-old Kay. The room, too, was a medium-sized square. One tall window on the north side and two on the west provided light. Like the rest of the house, the room had shiny wooden floors and varnished wood casings around the windows. A second set of sliding doors in the south wall led to the front entryway and the stairs to the second-floor quarters. Those sliding doors always remained shut, blocked by my mother's piano.

I quickly claimed the northwest corner as my own. That allowed me to have a window at each end of my bed. Most importantly, I could lie at the foot of my bed and look out at my beloved fir tree.

My heart was home, so the new house did not seem strange at all. By evening, my bed had been installed. I lay in the darkness listening to the sounds of the old house. I wanted to learn its creaks and moans, the character that all old houses possess.

I wanted to think about the happy times other people must have had there. I wanted to think about so much, but the sighing of the fir tree claimed me first. I slept.

FIRSTBORN

Winterset was the first town I can remember as a child. Although I had been born in the small Madison County Memorial Hospital, my parents lived outside a tiny town named Macksburg, seventeen miles southwest of Winterset.

As children do, I often begged my mother to recount the circumstances of my birth.

In April 1952, ten months after their marriage, Mom discovered she was pregnant. The nearly new bride wouldn't have minded waiting longer before a pregnancy had occurred. She was barely accustomed to her role as a wife. She suddenly had all the thrills of pregnancy, including morning sickness each day. She wasn't sure she was pleased with the situation.

My father spent days on the road with his job. Arriving home late Friday nights, he handed his dirty shirts to his new wife to wash, starch, and iron in time for him to leave Sunday evening. Their honeymoon period had been short before reality had settled into their lives.

That, however, was what young couples did in the early 1950s. They met, fell in love, married, and nature soon began the process of creating the new generation that would be called the baby boomers.

As time passed, the excitement did grow. The morning sickness eased, but Mom's appetite never really returned. She ate many mashed potatoes, one of the few foods that laid quietly in her often-queasy stomach.

My father became the typical expectant daddy. He

hated to leave for work and worried about her every day he was gone.

When late November arrived but the baby who would become me had not, my expectant mother was moved into a rooming house in Winterset. In winter weather, it was too risky to leave a pregnant woman alone in a farmhouse far from the hospital.

For one lonely month, my mother felt her baby grow and her spirits sink. With nothing to do and no friends nearby, Mom awaited the birth of her first baby.

The rooming house owner provided some companionship. Also, her parents-in-law, Grandpa Lyle and Grandma Mary, made the trip from Macksburg to see her as often as they could. They were still farming and, like most farmers, only went to town on Saturdays to shop and maybe on Sundays to visit or go to church.

Mom missed her own four brothers and her mother. The 120-mile one-way trip by car from their homes in northwest Missouri to Winterset was not practical on a regular basis. The roads to Missouri were two lanes with a fair number of curves. All of her brothers farmed, so leaving for a day meant they still had to be home by dark to milk and care for livestock. Since winter had arrived, ice and snowstorms could appear suddenly, and the chance of becoming unable to return home the same day was high.

Folks who traveled in December kept a close watch on the sky. Farmers could read the clouds and smell the wind to predict storms almost better than the weather forecasters.

Mom held on to the hope of an early delivery, although the thought of giving birth frightened her. Never having babysat for others and being the youngest in her family, she had little experience with babies or birthing.

Dad was traveling and spent the evening of December 18 in a hotel in Ottumwa, Iowa. The couple spoke on the telephone that evening, and Mom felt fine.

Finally, I decided December 19 was to be the day of my birth, so I started the process of escaping the womb. Around two o'clock in the morning, Mom began having labor pains. She called the same hotel, but the clerk then on duty said Dad was not registered there. Mom argued that they had spoken earlier, but the clerk said he could not find my father's name. Actually, Dad was present, but the clerk couldn't decipher his handwriting on the register.

At three o'clock as Mom was driven by taxi to the hospital, an ice storm hit Winterset and the surrounding area. The day of my birth proved one of those memorable days that chill the soul at the time but are somehow transformed into fond memories in later years.

I arrived before dawn on that icy Friday, December 19. Mom survived the ordeal well, but alone. Even if Dad had arrived, he would not have been allowed to be with her during the birth. In the 1950s, no one was allowed in the delivery room except the woman in pain, the baby to be, and the hospital staff.

Dad arrived in Winterset early Friday evening, sliding into town on ice-covered roads. As he crossed a downtown street, a friend from Macksburg hailed him. "You've got a new daughter at the hospital!"

Dad told him he must be joking, but the man insisted I had been born. The man was adamant. "My wife also had a baby girl last night!"

Dr. Chestnut had performed the delivery, although

Mom and I felt we did most of the work. I was another straightforward birth, like hundreds the doctor had overseen before.

Winterset boasted two doctors who had been there as long as most people could remember. The doctors had delivered most of the current residents of Winterset, their children, and even their grandchildren. They listened to people's troubles, thumped their chests, and sent them home with needed prescriptions. Medical school had taught them well, but common sense went further in those parts than fancy words and pills.

I imagine one or the other of those two men had seen every square inch of every citizen's body in Winterset. I reflected on that thought during one of my later, infrequent doctor visits. As a child, I felt that some bodies might be better left unexamined.

I shared the sense of comfort, however, that all Winterset residents had in being cared for by the same doctors all their lives. The two doctors, more than any other residents, saw the passing of time and history in Winterset.

THE NEIGHBORHOOD

I had to find my place in the new world called the neighborhood. I was four and a half, going on five, in the summer of 1957. My parents declared the neighborhood boundaries to be the west half of the block on which we lived, which consisted of two city blocks joined together into an east-west double block. The restriction meant that at all times I would be more or less within Mom's eyesight from some part of our yard. I could see places stretching beyond those imposed limits and wondered what adventures could be found there.

A model of true Iowa practicality, the flat town had been platted in a perfect grid system. Winterset's named streets ran sunrise to sunset, such as Court, Jefferson, and Buchanan. North and south streets were numbered and called "avenues" west of Main Street and "streets" on the east half of town. Our home was five blocks northeast of the courthouse square.

As I began to assess the situation, I decided to accept the boundaries, for now. I sensed that I could stretch them a bit later. Being rather assertive, even at my tender age, I guessed I could manage to change my parents' opinion when the time came.

The day after our move, I sat on the corner of the front porch. My arms were wrapped around my legs, my chin resting on my knees. Still early morning, few people were stirring. I didn't know people's names, so I classified them by appearance.

At the south end of the block, across the street from

the elementary school, sat a small two-story frame house. I later learned that the house belonged to the Albers family. The second floor had a sharply slanted roof. I wondered if the people sleeping upstairs often bumped their heads when they awoke each morning. The father left the house wearing a suit and carrying a briefcase. I judged him to be a businessman.

Next to that home was a one-story, stucco-covered house with high, thick, stucco-covered porch railings. An elderly lady, later introduced as Mrs. Wilson, came out and shook a throw rug. I concluded that house could be a potential source of trouble for me. I had been sternly warned by my parents not to annoy any elderly people in the neighborhood.

The house next to mine was a more modern design, unusual for the neighborhood. I recalled someone saying that an architect who had once lived there had designed the house. Now it belonged to the Ferguson family.

The sides of the house were covered in dull dark brown shingles. The yard grass was trimmed short, much shorter than my father liked to mow his. I heard the backdoor slam and the garage door open. Soon a car engine engaged, and a man in a suit slowly backed the car down the driveway. Another businessman, I noted.

Those were the houses on the west half of my block. Only two had garages—the one next door and the old woman's. That meant fewer places to explore. I sighed with disappointment.

Most of the trees I could see were hard maples or my beloved fir tree. The hard maples lined the entire length of our block along North Second Street. They all had their lower branches trimmed away. Thus, I couldn't climb them. Another sigh escaped me.

The brown house next door, however, had a smaller tree in the backyard. The tree reached about twenty feet high. Some kind of cable ran through it from my house to a pole at the southeast corner of the neighbor's yard. The pretty tree had small green cherries growing on the tips of its branches. A sturdy horizontal branch grew about four feet off the ground. That tree had potential.

The neighborhood began to stir. Cars passed by, heading for unknown places. Some drove cautiously. Some sped by too fast. I figured I could tell the kind of person who owned the car by its color and the way the person drove.

I noticed that red cars went by faster and had young brassy guys driving them. Cream-colored cars went by more slowly with older men behind the wheel. The man from the brown house had a cream-colored car. Owners of cream-colored cars were cautious and had no sense of adventure, I concluded.

As the early summer sun rose, I watched to see if any children lived nearby. The far south house had a boy and three girls. They appeared on the front porch, surveyed the morning scene, then disappeared back through their front door. The youngest girl looked about Kay's age of one and a half. The next older girl seemed between Kay's and my age of five and a half, with the brother and one sister older still. I ranked them possible playmates.

I could hear people stirring inside the brown house. Through the open bedroom windows, I could hear a girl whining, "I can't find my hairbrush." Another voice told her, "Open her eyes and look for it."

Then he emerged, a boy about three. He wore new-looking, store-bought shorts and matching shirt. His tawny blond hair was trimmed in the current butch style. His hair color nearly matched his pale skin tone. At a distance, it almost looked like he didn't have any hair at all.

The boy was Raymond Ferguson. As he shuffled out the door, his lack of energy, or boredom with the world, filled the yard. He poked the toe of his tennis shoe in the grass while he shoved his hands in his pockets.

I sat quite still. I liked having a chance to analyze people before they noticed my watching them. I assessed the boy as being like his father, not overly adventurous. He also seemed lonely. My instincts told me I could lead Raymond around like a puppy if I handled the situation right.

I waited until the boy finally looked up before I gave him a short wave of my wrist. He didn't look terribly surprised to see me.

He must have watched from inside his house as my family moved in the previous day. Unloading the trucks and hauling the boxes and furniture into the house had been a noisy affair. Also, my baby sister Kay had fallen out of her highchair and I had lost a tooth on moving day, so the activities had been rather chaotic. He must have heard the commotion.

He shuffled a couple of steps in my direction. I decided I was going to have to make the first move, or we were never going to start a friendship.

Unclasping my legs, I casually stretched myself out. I swung my body off the high porch, landing between two peony bushes. I walked two steps, picked up a small twig, and proceeded to examine it carefully. My feet managed to saunter over to the edge of the sidewalk that separated the two properties.

The boy dug his toe into a new section of grass a couple of feet beyond his initial point. Then he swung his other leg ahead to another spot and continued to ease in my direction.

Finally, we faced each other across the sidewalk barrier between our properties. He continued to poke holes in the ground. I began pulling thin strips of bark off the green twig. Our first conversation went somewhat along these lines.

"Hi," one said.

"Hi," came the reply.

He was not much of a conversationalist. The meeting needed a little momentum.

"I like your cherry tree," I said.

His thin shoulders twitched in a small shrug. "It's okay."

He spotted a deep-purple-colored beetle and squashed it soundly.

I grabbed a larger section of bark and gave it a good jerk. "Ever climb it?" I tossed out.

His downcast eyes peeked over his right shoulder, then returned to the ground. "Yeah, sometimes."

"Want to now?" I suggested.

Another peek at the tree and another stab at the dirt followed. "Sure, why not."

Another long-lasting Winterset friendship had just been established.

We two children sauntered and shuffled our way toward the tree. Suddenly, a silent challenge made us break into a full run to see who could reach the tree, and the best perch, first. I let Raymond win. He owned the tree. There would be plenty of other times for me to beat him.

THE GRANDPARENTS

When I was young, I had two living grandmothers and one living grandfather. The situation was off-balanced, but many situations in life are.

My maternal grandfather, who had passed away when Mom was fifteen, had been named Doug. I learned that, as a Missouri farmer, he had little time for frivolity. When the weather was clear, he planted or disked or harvested his crops.

Sundays, however, were the Lord's day, so a farmer didn't work that day except in an emergency. Sometimes when the hay had been cut and dried, but not yet baled, the forecasters might predict severe rains the following day. Then a farmer had to work or face economic disaster from a lost crop. In that case, a farmer felt the Lord should understand his situation and not hold it against him if he missed church. After all, the Lord sent the coming rainstorm, so he ought to be compassionate toward the farmer.

Sunday was the one day the men of the 1950s spent time with their families. Families attended church in the morning, ate a Sunday dinner at noon, and often had outings in the afternoon.

When Mom was a child in Missouri, the family might have a long-delayed picnic or travel to visit nearby friends. The annual town picnic and small traveling carnival might start on a Friday night and continue through the following weekend, with Sundays being chances for afternoon family fun. Major events usually occurred on Sundays.

One such holy day had arrived when Mom was a young girl in Missouri. A too-warm summer's breeze drifting through the elm trees did little to relieve the heat. That day was perfect for a town-wide baseball game. Any male old enough to swing a bat was invited.

Mom's family was out in force. She and her mother made a picnic lunch. Her four brothers and their father gathered their baseball gloves.

The residents of the small town of Barnard rounded up enough men and boys to form two teams, with a few reserves. The younger male farmers tended to enjoy roughhousing along the baselines, so minor injuries sometimes occurred; no padded safety gear existed for local sports games. Thus, most of the men eventually had a chance to play.

Farming would just be done more slowly the next day, while bodies ached and healed. The women understood and always kept the liniment handy for the after-the-game rubdowns. Their husbands were too old to be competing in sports against teenage boys.

Grandfather Doug served as umpire. He had a reputation for being fair, even when it came to the pranks of his own boys. He dealt out reprimands and punishment when they were deserved. He handed out praise the same way.

The game was nearly over. Just another inning remained. His sons' team was behind but catching up. The lanky young pitcher could fire in a fastball as easily as he lifted a bale of hay.

The ball he threw sped toward home plate. Somehow the catcher blinked and totally missed the ball. The baseball slammed into Grandpa Doug's groin.

As Doug crashed to the ground in pain, his family rushed to his side. Minutes passed before he could breathe regularly again. As with most farmers who had injuries, he waved off attempts at aid. He walked off the worst of the pain, then finished the game.

No one ever thought about calling a doctor. Injuries happened all the time while farming, and people usually treated themselves. Besides, doctors cost money, and all my grandfather had was a good-sized bruise, not worth the expense of a doctor.

A few years later, however, Grandpa Doug died from a tumor in his groin. The family always wondered if the baseball injury was related to his later illness.

My widowed Grandma Effie carried on without him. She kept the farm for a while but finally sold it. As with most widows, Grandma bought a small house in town, first in Maryville and later in Barnard, where she planted a garden and tended her wrens. She never remarried. Her boys looked after her and visited whenever they stopped in town for supplies. After Mom married and moved to Iowa, she saw her mother when she could. Grandma Effie lived as she chose for over forty more years.

* * *

Both my father's parents were alive when I was young. They had married just after the turn of the century. A rarity for the time, Grandpa Lyle had attended Simpson College in Indianola, Iowa, over fifty miles from home.

The neighbors thought it was mighty uppity for a farm boy to go to college. Everything he really needed to know could be learned from his father. Great-grandpa Morley, however, saw how farming was changing and wanted something more for his only child.

While in college, Grandpa Lyle had to work several jobs to pay for tuition. His father sent him to college but didn't have the money to pay for all the expenses.

The thrill of learning and reading never left Grandpa. He practiced hours at one of the required courses, penmanship, until he had mastered the flourishing strokes of beautiful handwriting.

Grandpa Lyle also mastered the heart of a local girl. Mary was the daughter of a Methodist circuit rider and had six brothers and sisters. A petite woman, Grandma possessed the most graceful hands he had ever seen. With her button nose, she looked exceptionally appealing when she smiled, as she often did whenever she saw Grandpa coming up the walk.

They married shortly after Grandpa graduated from college. After the wedding service, they drove off in a buggy, dragging behind the ceremonial shoes and tin cans.

Home was a small house at the entrance to the lane on his father's homestead farm. Morley's own house, at the upper end of the lane, was far enough away for privacy but close enough for Grandpa to join his father before heading to the fields each day.

Grandma helped her mother-in-law Phoebe gather eggs and tend the large vegetable garden. In season, they picked berries, dug potatoes, and canned vegetables and meat.

As the years passed and his parents died, Grandpa and Grandma moved into the main house. Their honeymoon home was sold and moved to a new location ten miles from Grandpa's farm. All I ever saw were the original foundation stones.

* * *

I was carried home to Macksburg from the Winterset hospital the day before Christmas 1952. For some reason, Grandpa and Grandma expected Mom to cook the Christmas dinner the next day. She still felt weak and didn't need the pressure of such an undertaking so soon after giving birth. But she did it.

My parents' home was a small, one-story, four-room cottage down the hill, across the valley, and on top of the next rise east from my grandparents' house. Our living room had a large picture window that overlooked my grandparents' place. Fir trees formed windbreaks along the north and west sides of their home. The morning animal sounds floated in the still air from the barn on the east across an open area from their house. All I could glimpse of the main house was the roof, for elm and oak trees blocked the view.

Dad continued traveling with his job. That left Mom and me, the sprouting child, alone a great deal. We were busy enough with my pranks and Mom's gardening to pass the time. Mom always talked to me in a grownup manner, rather than cooing baby talk. I loved to bang the pots and pans with a wooden spoon. Many days, however, were long and lonely.

Our only regular visitor was Grandpa Lyle. Every morning after initial chores, Grandpa eased his pickup or tractor down his lane, turned left, and headed up the road for our cottage. He came under the pretext of seeing if Mom was all right. We all knew, however, that he came to see his first grandchild who lived in Iowa. He had four other grandchildren by his eldest son, who lived in Utah, but rarely got to see them.

I became the twinkling light in Grandpa's eyes. He was my hero in overalls. I am told that, as soon as breakfast was over, my stubby legs stumbled toward the living room window. I remained in position until Grandpa came into view. Bubbling syllables, as yet indistinguishable as words, I spewed out my excitement. My grandpa was coming!

Grandpa and I sat on the porch or explored the barnyard for hours. Grandpa was almost retired and now raised only hay, a small area of grain crops, and some cattle. That suited him just fine, because it left time for his grandchild.

Grandpa and I hadn't read the psychology reports on the importance of multi-generational contact. We only knew that we were two kindred souls, by blood and by spirit, who thrived in each other's presence. We continued that way for decades to come.

THE PIANO

Mom had three dreams in her life: to earn a college degree, to buy a new car, and to learn to play the piano. She accomplished all of them.

Mother bought the Storey and Clark upright piano in Maryville, Missouri, during the late 1940s when she was in her twenties. The piano was one of her most cherished possessions.

She saved the money from her salary as a teacher at one-room country schoolhouses near Maryville and Barnard. She earned the sum of around $100 per month for the nine-month school year, from which she also had to deduct her living expenses.

She brought the piano to the small house in Maryville that she shared with her widowed mother. When Mom married Dad in June 1951, she moved the piano to their first home, the small house on Grandpa's farm outside Macksburg, Iowa.

In January 1953, she moved the Storey and Clark to a small house next to the Methodist Church parsonage in Macksburg. The next move my parents made in 1954 was to a larger rented home, also in Macksburg.

When our family arrived in Winterset in 1957, the treasured piano came along. The musical instrument stood proudly along the south wall of the bedroom Kay and I shared. The bedroom had less furniture than the living room, so there was room for the piano.

The polished medium-brown wood reflected the late afternoon sunsets shining through the two windows. The gold foil Storey and Clark emblem, looking like the royal crest of a proud piano company, gleamed in the center of the keyboard cover.

When Kay and I were young, Mom's piano playing was part of our bedtime routine. First, a necessary bath removed the dirt and sweat from a hard day's play activities. Next, we slipped into our nightly attire, sleeveless cotton gowns for summer or two-piece flannel pajamas for winter.

We took turns all sitting on Kay's bed one night and my bed the next while Mom read us bedtime stories. The Fuzzy Little Puppy and Farm Babies were favorite tales when I was young, I was told. Later, Dr. Seuss had us laughing at his rhymes and nonsensical words. Although both Kay and I could read at an early age, the stories were more memorable when listening to the soothing tone of Mom's voice.

After reading our storybooks, we snuggled into bed. In summer, it was so warm we only laid a cotton sheet over our feet to keep the fan's draft from chilling our toes. My parents believed that children caught cold if their feet laid in a draft at night. In winter, we burrowed under the sheets topped with handmade quilts until we felt like hibernating bears in cozy caves.

Mother then approached the piano. She pulled out the long, rectangular, four-legged piano bench from its daytime spot nestled beneath the keyboard. She lifted the bench lid and select several pieces of sheet music.

Closing the lid, Mom placed the sheet music on the piano rack. Then she positioned the bench back from the piano. Mom was quite tall, and she needed a lot of room between the piano and the bench for her long legs. Next she sat on the bench, making final positioning adjustments.

Flexing her fingers, Mom made her first musical selection by opening a folded sheet of music. She studied the first few notes to refresh her memory about the song's key and tempo. She had to rely on the room's ceiling light and a small lamp clamped onto the piano lid for illumination.

Mother tentatively positioned her hands above the keys. Then she began to play the long-familiar tunes.

In summer, she often played "Bell Bottom Trousers," "Missouri Waltz," "Dear Hearts and Gentle People," and one of my personal favorites, "Far Away Places." Other tunes included "Mockingbird Hill," "The Oklahoma Waltz," and "Bells of St. Mary's." Around Christmas, she played "Santa Claus Is Coming to Town," "Frosty the Snowman," "Silver Bells," and my all-time favorite song, "White Christmas."

Many of the songs had been written in the 1930s and 40s. Mom had purchased the sheet music when she had been in her twenties. Each time she moved, the piano and the sheet music always came along, both carefully wrapped to avoid damage.

After teaching school and grading papers all day, caring for two girls in the early evening, and reading bedtime stories, Mom's eyes were tired by nightfall. She managed to play only two or three tunes before the notes looked fuzzy to her and her eyelids started to close from exhaustion.

Mom's playing ability could be classified as average. She had never been able to take enough lessons to become as skilled a pianist as she desired to be. Lessons cost precious dollars, always in short supply. Practice time was also at a premium after teaching school and caring for her family.

Her ability, however, mattered little to Kay and me. Mom played because she enjoyed doing so. She played from her heart, out of her love of music. Playing the piano was the one hobby in life she did to please herself.

Being four years younger, Kay often fell asleep before Mom finished playing. Her bed was next to the piano, so the music's volume totally blocked any outside street noises for her. The music quickly lulled her to sleep.

I lay in my bed, listening quietly. Word fragments from the bedtime stories floated through my mind, intermingled with the lyrics of the songs being played. Eventually, all of the mental images and music began to blur. I became so sleepy that I could not force my eyes to remain open. The weight of the blankets held my body in a warm embrace. I slept.

Mom finished her third piece. I sometimes awakened slightly and peeked through barely lifted eyelids. I saw Mom carefully gather her sheet music, returning it inside the piano bench. She slowly pushed the bench under the piano, being careful not to make any loud noises that might awaken her supposedly sleeping daughters.

She flipped off the bedroom light switch by the doorway. Looking at us, she pulled the door closed so only a slight opening remained. I knew she would peek in on us a few more times before going to bed herself. I also knew my world was secure for another night.

THE CATS

All children should experience the joys and responsibilities of owning a pet. Animals teach empathy for other creatures and bring enduring companionship. They provide unquestioning love and devotion, sensing our emotions of sadness or joy.

My parents told me that I had a small white dog when we lived in the small house east of Grandpa's farm. I do not remember it, and it died from rabies when I was young. Farmers did not spend money on rabies shots for pets back in the mid-1950s. Pets lived or died as circumstances happened.

One night as Kay and I headed to bed, Dad came home earlier than usual. He carried a medium-sized box under one arm, from which noises emitted. Curious, Kay and I detoured to the kitchen instead of our bedroom.

When Dad opened the box lid, two tiny black bundles of fur blinked at the lights. Reaching inside, my father lifted out one kitten, then the other. They were adorable, warm and cuddly, and scared of their new surroundings. A client in Des Moines had a cat with a litter of kittens, and Dad accepted a brother and sister combo to bring home to Winterset.

Mom knew nothing about the impending arrival of those additions to the family. We had no litter box, cat food, or toys for them After a discussion, it was decided that the two kittens could survive until morning on a little milk. Dad took a short wooden crate and filled it with some soil from a flower bed to serve as a litter box.

The moment Kay and I laid eyes on the kittens, no one could have gotten them away from us. We now had living toys to enjoy instead of dolls and teddy bears. We hugged and petted them, welcoming them to their new home.

Another family conference resulted in names for the two: Midnight and Teena. Obviously, his black coloring accounted for Midnight's name. Teena was also all black except for a small, white, upside-down triangular patch over her breastbone. The kittens were half-Siamese, so their ears were more pointed than other cats.

Mom soon declared that the cats had to sleep in the basement at night. A box with blankets provided a bed, and the litter box was placed nearby. Reluctantly, Kay and I said good night to the cats and headed for bed.

Within a few days, the kittens had surveyed their new territory from top to bottom. Dad made a toy using a long piece of twine tied around a rolled up narrow section of newspaper. The kittens chased and pounced on the newspaper as Kay and I pulled the twine around the room. Soon the paper was shredded, and we had to make another section for them to chase.

The two kittens had distinct personalities. Teena proved to be a lady with wonderful manners who quickly learned the house rules of behavior. Midnight was all boy, whether human or animal, full of nonstop energy and speed. He raced through the house, darting from room to room in exuberance. Only when he had exhausted his last ounce of energy did he take a nap.

Even though we lived on a relatively quiet street with modest traffic loads, Mom wanted the kittens to stay indoors. She could not bear the thought of coming home from teaching school with us girls to find a cat flattened on the road under some car's tread. The cats didn't seem to mind being confined inside since they received so much attention from us girls.

Midnight's manners did not improve. As an indoor cat, he was a disaster. During one racing session, he sprinted through the kitchen and into the living room. Climbing more than halfway up Mother's sheer drapes, he shredded a large section as he clung to the fabric with his claws and his body weight sliced down the surface. That was the last straw. Mother had had enough.

But even she did not want Midnight to be shoved outside to live as an outdoor cat. His mother had been an indoor cat, and Midnight's first few months had been indoors. After a discussion with my grandparents, they agreed to keep him as an inside cat on their farm. If he happened to slip outside, at least no cars would endanger his life.

Kay and I hated to see Midnight go, even though we understood the reasons. At least we could visit him when we saw our grandparents.

Dad took Midnight to the farmhouse, where his manners did not improve. My grandparents' small house had the rooms arranged in a circle. One room lead to another and another and back to the first room. After Midnight had used the layout for a raceway for the several thousandth time, Grandma Mary said he had to go. She had rheumatoid arthritis and could not chase down a sprinting cat.

Now Kay and I were truly concerned over what would become of Midnight. He had gained several pounds and was obviously healthy from his energetic lifestyle. He just needed a home that fit his personality.

The next and final stop became the farm of Mom's oldest brother Robert. My uncle lived outside Barnard, Missouri, and farmed a good-sized tract of land. The farm became Midnight's final chance.

Kay and I continued to enjoy Teena's company and antics. She kept us entertained and guarded us like she would her own kittens. We still worried, however, about Midnight and what would become of him.

After several months, Uncle Rob reported to Mom that Midnight had taken over the farm and all its possessions. He had grown into an eighteen-pound king of the homestead, easily taking on all encroaching tom cats and handily dispatching them to distant territories. Outdoors was his domain, and he guarded it with pride and jealousy. Nothing messed with Midnight.

Our cats taught Kay and me that other creatures had personalities, wants, and needs. One could be gracious and ladylike, while her brother could be a true hellcat. We learned to clean the litter box, although Mom probably scooped more than we did. We learned to feed the cat, because Teena did not let us have any peace or eat our own supper until she had been properly tended. She taught us how to play nicely with her and how to read her moods. Teena was always gentle with us girls, never deliberately hurting us. She did take great pleasure in being able to jump out from behind furniture to scare us into small shrieks of surprise.

Kay and I also learned that pets die. We never knew how long Midnight lived, although it was more years than most outdoor cats survive. Our Teena lived to nearly fourteen years old before she left us for the last time. Such is the circle of life.

SATURDAY MORNING TELEVISION

For me, Saturday was the best day of the week. On that day, I did not have to rush off to school or church. Saturday was the one day I was allowed to watch a substantial amount of television.

I was almost seven in the fall of 1959 when our family bought its first used television set. The old Motorola was made of wood stained a medium-dark brown and was shaped like a large box two and a half feet wide and deep, and about three feet high.

Mom had not wanted to spend the money on a television set. As her fourth-grade school students talked about things they saw on TV, however, Mom soon began to feel she was left out of the latest innovations and news. She finally relented to purchase the television.

Inside, vacuum tubes lit up when the television was operating. I could just peek at them through circular perforations in the set's fiberboard backing. On the front were two knobs: one for turning on the set and one for changing the channels. Our four channel choices were ABC, NBC, CBS, and PBS. For me, the black and white screen displayed eighteen diagonal inches of pure Hollywood delight.

My sister and I rarely watched movies because they usually appeared on television in the evenings after our bedtime. The one exception was The Wizard of Oz, which had premiered in theaters in 1939. One of the four local broadcasting stations aired the movie every year on a March Saturday night.

Our television set had one major quirk. It instinctively knew when The Wizard of Oz was going to be aired each March. For several years, the television broke down one to two weeks before the Saturday night that the movie was to be shown. Depending on whether spare money was available to fix the cantankerous television provided the key to our spring happiness. If we were lucky, Mom had the funds and called Mr. Clark to repair the latest tube breakdown.

Television programming in the late 1950s was still in its infancy. Many evening shows were performed live, so neither the actors, hosts, sponsors, nor audience could ever be sure what would occur or if the script would be followed as written or ad-libbed. The scariest program was "The Twilight Zone" hosted by Rod Sterling, a show I was never allowed to watch because my parents feared it would cause me to have nightmares.

Saturday morning programming for children, however, proved entirely wholesome. While I often found it difficult to rise during the week for school, I had no problem being up and dressed and eating my breakfast before my Saturday morning series of shows began.

I started the morning at 8:30 with Mighty Mouse, the strongest rodent that ever flew across the screen to catch lawbreakers. At 9:00, The Lone Ranger and Tonto always got the bad guys. My Friend Flicka at 9:30 developed my love of horses, like the quarter horses my uncles owned. At 10:00, Sky King taught me to love airplanes before I had ever ridden in one or even seen one up close.

The best show, however, was Roy Rogers at 10:30. No one was allowed to interrupt me during Roy Rogers' appearances. My eyes were glued to the television screen, wishing I were riding with him full gallop across the Western landscape chasing rustlers.

I laughed at the antics of his sidekick Pat and wondered how he managed to drive his jeep Nellie-Belle so haphazardly without crashing it more often. I wished Dale Evans would be allowed to be a heroine more often, but I figured since the name of the show was Roy Rogers then he had to be the hero most of the episodes.

I could sing along to "Happy Trails to You" before I knew the lyrics to most other tunes. The song was so important to me that I rarely missed the opening or closing credits so I could hear the music twice in one morning. Then the tune continued to rumble through my head throughout the week.

The only other song that affected me as greatly was a song on the 3:30 p.m. weekday show, The Mickey Mouse Club. That was the song in which Jimminy Cricket spelled out "E-N-C-Y-C-L-O-P-E-D-I-A." I first learned to spell that long word, and never missed spelling it in school, because of that song.

The Roy Rogers show always taught that the hero wins in the end. No matter how mean, ornery, or law-breaking the outlaws were, Roy rounded 'em up in half an hour each Saturday morning.

The good guys always wore white hats, and Roy and Dale both had white horses, at least they appeared white on a black-and-white television set. I decided that Roy and Pat wore white hats so it was easier to spot them during the chase scenes when the dust was flying from the galloping horses' hooves. Oftentimes, their hats did not even fall off during the ensuing fisticuffs when Roy and Pat finally caught up with the outlaws.

A miracle always occurred during the fight scenes. Even if an outlaw slugged Roy with a hard right cross,

Roy never had a black eye or a bruise when the show ended. The criminals always looked beaten up, however, when Roy finished with them.

Roy Rogers set high moral standards for America's youth in the late 1950s and early 1960s. Roy always told the truth, stood by his friends, never said a mean word about anyone, and was kind to his horses and dog Bullet. He kept his word, even if it took him the entire show to carry out his promise. Whenever he met a stranger, Roy appeared kind, considerate, and helpful, unless he discovered the stranger was a bank robber or rustler.

Even off the television screen, Roy Rogers and Dale Evans practiced in their lives the standards they portrayed through their fictional characters. They adopted several children, lost their only biological child to an early death, and lived an upright life.

Years later, I got to see Roy Rogers in person perform as a singer and cowboy doing rope tricks and riding his horse Trigger at the Iowa State Fair. Seeing him was one of the greatest thrills for me. During the show, I bought a souvenir program about his performance, the first such booklet I had ever purchased. I still have it as a treasured memento of a man who portrayed the ideals of my youth.

AUNT GENEVIEVE

Aunt Genevieve always arrived in a flurry of style seldom seen in my Iowa hometown during the 1950s. She was the first person I knew who had a mink collar on her wool winter coat.

Aunt Genevieve was my grandaunt, one of four sisters in my paternal grandmother's family. As Grandma Mary's older sister, she received the authority that seniority traditionally accorded.

Aunt Genevieve and Uncle Bailey lived in California. They usually made an annual trek to Iowa to visit her sister Mary and other relatives in the Midwest.

Her announced arrival date in the fall of 1959 meant my mother did a thorough housecleaning, including a head-to-toe bathing of nearly three-year-old Kay and nearly seven-year-old me. Orders to behave ourselves and act like young ladies were issued, but unnecessary. Aunt Genevieve's presence always left me in awe.

Always a lady herself, Aunt Genevieve never acted superior. Her presence through posture, grooming, stylish clothes, and quiet manner carried her into a room.

I lacked most of those qualities and could only gaze in wonder at her. My parents constantly reminded me that I should aspire to act more like a lady. I never could, usually being too spirited to sit still very long and preferring tomboy activities.

My favorite aspect of Aunt Genevieve involved none of those finer points of womanhood. I loved Aunt Genevieve because she always insisted on taking my grandparents and all of my family out to dinner at the fanciest restaurant in Winterset—the Gold Buffet. Her trips were the only time each year we ate at that well-known establishment.

The Gold Buffet opened in Winterset in the 1958. The man who would become the owner lived in Van Meter and had been looking for a business to start. When he asked his friends which businesses made money, they replied, "Food and bowling." Thus, he built the Gold Buffet with half as a bowling alley and half as a formal buffet restaurant, with a snack bar between the two. The Gold Buffet was the only restaurant in town with tablecloths and linen napkins.

People from all over central Iowa traveled to Winterset just to enjoy the Gold Buffet's wonderful and extensive food selections. The restaurant was so successful that a later owner opened a second location in Kansas City, Missouri.

As I child, I had never seen so much food already cooked and waiting for a hungry youngster who could eat herself into a stomachache. Salads rested in silver bowls atop crushed ice. Several varieties of soup steamed in large black kettles. The main table held more entrees than could possibly be sampled in one meal. As a bonus, a man in a white chef's hat and coat carved large slices of roast beef, ham, and other first-quality meats.

My heart, however, really belonged to Aunt Genevieve because she always insisted that we girls have a finishing treat. Dessert was the only part of a meal I considered as precious as life itself, and it was not included in the buffet price. Aunt Genevieve had to pay extra for us to enjoy those delectable bites.

The Gold Buffet had a dessert cart pushed by a waitress in a short black dress with a white lacy apron. From the cart, I could choose pecan pie, chocolate cream pie, puddings, or other rich taste temptations. I only beheld so many miracles of culinary delight that one day each year when Aunt Genevieve visited.

Because of the honor she bestowed upon me by allowing me such desserts, I naturally wanted to return my gratitude. Thus, my parents never had to closely supervise me. I never dreamed of misbehaving during her visit and possibly missing the taste bud adventures that awaited me. I even quietly consented to wearing my best, starchy, itchy dress for the occasion.

Years passed, but I never grew into as refined a lady as my Aunt Genevieve represented. The buffet portion of the Gold Buffet finally closed, to the detriment of those who enjoyed fine formal dining in Winterset. Aunt Genevieve and Uncle Bailey became too old to make the long trip to Iowa each year.

I, however, never lost my appreciation for gracious dining that I first learned from Aunt Genevieve. I will always love anticipating a special occasion, donning dressy attire, and gliding into a formal dining room feeling my best.

Aunt Genevieve, your style and zest for life live on in my memories.

COUNTRY STARLIGHT

The children's poem "Twinkle, Twinkle Little Star" is best understood when standing outside beneath the starry heavens. In the late 1950s, our family trips to the Iowa countryside taught me to appreciate the night's darkness, not fear it, because of country starlight.

One of our family traditions was having Sunday lunch with my grandparents as often as possible. We often made the seventeen-mile drive from Winterset to their farmhouse outside Macksburg after Sunday morning church services.

Mother brought along some food dishes, one of which usually included green beans, not one of my favorites. Grandma Mary cooked potatoes, either boiled or mashed. Sunday dinner in Iowa was complete only with meat-and-potatoes farm cooking.

After we arrived, Kay and I amused ourselves by exploring the old barn or playing with Lassie, Grandpa's black-and-white collie. Grandma tried to teach us the names of all the bird species around their farm. We could hear the bobwhites calling to their mates in the late afternoon shadows. Kay could mimic the bobwhite's call, often carrying on extended conversations with the birds.

Frequently, we stayed for supper. Afterwards, Kay and I tried to catch fireflies in our hands. We never harmed them; we merely enjoyed watching their tails blinking through the cracks among our fingers. Their earthly flashing lights lit the yard like the blinking stars lit the night skies.

By the time we began the drive back to Winterset, night cloaked the countryside in near total darkness. In the 1950s, most farms had only a single light bulb on a pole for illuminating the barnyard area after dark. By nine o'clock, farmers turned off their yard lights to save the cost of electricity, blackening the entire countryside.

Dad drove the car, with Mom sitting in the front passenger seat. Kay was usually propped against Mom's shoulder. Sometimes she laid her head in Mom's lap, where she quickly fell asleep. I stretched out in the back seat.

The return trip to town was one of my favorite parts of the day. With the countryside darkened, the stars blinked brightly in the heavens.

I gazed out the rear car window, watching the stars. I tried to locate the Big and Little Dippers, the only constellations I knew. All the stars shone so brightly that they seemed close to the ground. I felt I could stretch my arm out the car's window and touch them with my hand. They winked, flashed, and glowed, making the night's darkness seem much friendlier.

As the car rounded a curve, the stars appeared to swivel in the sky. Dad seemed to rotate the heavens just by turning the car's steering wheel. On a winding road, I enjoyed the sensation of the stars constantly spinning overhead.

In town, we could see the stars, but even the dim streetlights diminished their brilliance. Only the view of them from the darkened open countryside showed their brightest glittering.

Modern street lighting in today's cities makes evening stars look like distant, dim, Christmas bulbs. Most farms and ranches have mercury vapor lights that burn all night, so even the countryside is rarely in total darkness any longer.

Children everywhere should have the chance to watch the night stars spin outside a car's window or to find the constellations. They should have the chance to appreciate the warm magic of country starlight.

THE PUBLIC LIBRARY:
THE LOCAL INFORMATION HIGHWAY

Reading has always been one of my greatest joys. At an early age, I discovered I could escape the real world and travel through time and space by exploring books.

During summers in the late 1950s, few organized summer recreational programs for children existed in Winterset. We children had to invent neighborhood games, read books, go to the city swimming pool, watch what few television programs were available (and allowed by our parents), and try our best to avoid becoming trapped into doing household chores.

Mom took us to the library about every two weeks. We checked out enough books to last for the allowed lending period, then carried them home. That meant an eight-block walk one way from our house to the library, located southwest of the courthouse square.

The Winterset Public Library was constructed for $10,000 through a grant from the Andrew Carnegie Foundation. In June 1905, the library opened with 4,000 volumes.

The properly serious edifice of the Winterset Public Library dominated the southeast corner of Court Street and Second Avenue. The building was rectangular, with a lower portion of rough-hewn limestone blocks and an upper half of dark red bricks.

I remember walking up several limestone steps that led to the large front doors. Once inside, the aroma of musty books and furniture polish immediately assailed my nostrils.

Inside the front door was a small landing. Archival books were stored downstairs in the basement, but I never knew anyone except the librarians who had ever been allowed to go there. The main library floor was half a story above ground level. To reach it, I had to climb more steep steps covered in red linoleum with a silver metal edging. The steps creaked loudly as I climbed, as though to alert the librarians to watch for visitors.

At the top of the stairs, I always paused momentarily to catch my breath after the steep ascent. With a child's short legs, I found the high steps difficult to traverse.

Next, I pushed open one of the two tall, swinging, wooden doors with large glass panels and brass push plates that led into the library. Directly in front of me rose the librarians' checkout desk as tall as a child's head.

Throughout the library, highly polished medium-dark wood had been constructed into shelves, pillars, door casings, and window frames. I could see my reflection as I walked past the wood sections.

To the left, the room contained children's books. I ran my finger along the book spines, reading the titles that awaited me. When I was younger, my favorite was anything by Dr. Seuss. Later, my preferences were the series about the Hardy Boys, Tom Swift, and the Black Stallion. I never cared for the Nancy Drew books because they did not have enough action adventure.

I had always wanted to wander around the rest of the library. On the same floor, three other areas contained books for reference, teenagers, and adults. The librarians, however, never allowed younger children to explore those possibilities.

When I made my new selections, I proceeded to the checkout desk staffed by two rather serious librarians. The wooden desk was an imposing structure, four feet high in a large U-shape. As a child, I had to stand on my tiptoes to lay my desired books on top of the desk for processing. The librarians always stared at me and firmly stated the return due date. I assumed their serious tone was meant to convey the awesome responsibility of checking out public library books.

As I grew older, I was allowed to walk to the library by myself. I ascended the stairs, then was immediately confronted by the continuously watchful eyes of the librarians the entire time I was in the library. Children were expected to behave in a calm quiet manner while in the library. Talking above a whisper was not permitted.

The librarians were always women in their early to late fifties and sixties, with sober countenances. They rarely smiled when a child checked out a book, especially a child not accompanied by an adult.

One day, while I wandered through the appropriate children's section, I noticed that the town library played another role in society. In a small town like Winterset with just under 3,500 people, the telephone was indispensable in disseminating local news. As I discovered, however, the public library was the second most popular source of information.

One at a time, throughout the summer morning, ladies of retirement age entered the library. Each returned a book, selected a new one, then proceeded to the checkout desk. To my amazement, the librarians smiled at each woman.

The next few moments were spent with a woman

patron exchanging details about area events and family happenings with the librarians. Once all relevant facts had been exchanged, the patron left. A few minutes later, another woman appeared, and the process started over again.

Through observing the rapid exchange of local news, I realized that any noteworthy events were reported all over town by noon each day. Each library patron who owned a telephone soon called her friends with the latest tidbits of news, as I knew various neighbors to do.

When I became an adult, I also realized spreading local information formed a way for people to apply peer pressure on other citizens. People in small towns tend to conform to expected standards of socially acceptable behavior to avoid becoming the subjects of gossip. The speed with which any deviation from the norm is noted by those on local news grapevines helps ensure such activity rarely occurs or, at least, occurs in extreme privacy. While some people might want to ignore public opinion, small town society tends to create an atmosphere of conformity to promote community cohesiveness.

The main advantage of public information, however, is that positive peer pressure can create a climate in which children and adults learn what is expected of them. The community can become a safer place when there are few secrets about personal lives. People are encouraged to obey the law, whether moral or legal, or risk exposure by the small-town information highway.

THE FORT

Western movies were still in their heyday in the late 1950s. John Wayne has always been my favorite cowboy star with his slow drawl and easy ambling gait. The fact that John Wayne was born Marion Robert Morrison in Winterset, Iowa, in 1907 probably helped my opinion of him. Just because his family moved from Iowa to California when he was quite young did not matter. He was still a Winterset native.

Ray, the boy next door, was five and I was seven years old the summer of 1960. As children who loved western movies, we knew we had to build a fort. The most important factor for a fort was its strategic location, because geography played a key role in a strong defense.

Ray's family had a detached two-car garage sitting about fifty feet east of his house. Along his south property line bounding Mrs. Wilson's yard was a row of tall bushes. The bushes extended to the back of Ray's property, passing next to the garage.

We decided the best place for our fort was between the bushes and the garage. The garage was, thereafter, referred to as the hill behind the fort. The bushes became the tree trunks that formed the fort's walls.

Ray and I found a few gardening tools inside his garage. With those, we dug a pit about four feet long, three feet wide, and one foot deep as the fort's central parade grounds. Here we crouched, defending our fort from all attackers.

At that point, we encountered one mathematical

problem. There were only two of us. Thus, we could both be soldiers defending the fort, or one could be a soldier and the other an Indian or rustler, or we could both be Indians. Our neighborhood was a little short on troop recruits, with Kay being too young and his two sisters too old, or at least, too grown up in their minds, to play with us.

We varied our choices, depending on our mood each morning when we began the game. Sometimes we two soldiers fought off assaults by imaginary attackers all day. Other times, when I played the Indian, the Indians always won. I was a head taller than Ray and more assertive. I was not about to lose the battle to one small soldier.

The issue of race relations never entered our minds as we played. We were just two small children emulating the cinematic world as we knew it.

Some days we two soldiers defended against a lengthy siege by the opposition. Our food supplies ran low. One of us had to volunteer bravely to sneak into enemy territory to steal some food.

Since Ray's mother was more lenient about between-meal snacks, Ray volunteered for the mission. While I fired off extra imaginary gun volleys, Ray sneaked across the wasteland between our fort and the enemy's camp inside his house. He zigzagged his way through the treacherous terrain, firing his imaginary finger gun at his enemies. Finally, he reached the fringes of the enemy's camp and slid through the doorway into the house.

Ray's return to the fort was even more hazardous. Now he had both hands full of cookies, otherwise known as hardtack biscuits by us soldiers. He could not fire his gun to defend himself. Thus, I had to fire out the front of the fort to ward off our attackers and behind me to defend Ray's return to the fort. Luckily, I was the fastest gun in our neighborhood.

If Ray had done his job quietly and well, the enemy did not even notice his presence. We tried to time the assault on the enemy's food supplies so Ray's mother was working in the living room, upstairs, or out in the front yard. We believed in sneak attacks.

Ray's valiant efforts always saved the fort's defenders from mid-afternoon starvation. The fort always closed at night when some of the fort's enemies, our mothers, called us home for supper and bedtime.

We two small soldiers defended our fort against whatever enemies appeared. We were brave, resourceful, and kind to the pretend wagon trains of settlers heading west to more adventures than we could possibly imagine in our small backyard fort. Our territory became the safest portion of the American westward expansion trail.

SWIMMING LESSONS

I began to take swimming lessons in the summer of 1960. Swimming was the first sports activity for which I had an instructor.

At one time, Winterset had a community pool on the southeast side of town. The area, however, received jolts several days a week by the vibrations from blasting at a rock quarry farther outside town. The quarry tended to use larger dynamite charges than should have been recommended.

Almost all the houses in the east half of town had cracks in their basements from the mini earthquakes caused by the quarry's blasting activities. The swimming pool had suffered the same fate. The city fathers found it difficult to maintain a prescribed water level in a swimming pool that had at least one crack down its side.

A citywide bond election was held, and funds for a new pool on the western edge of Winterset on Jefferson Street were approved. In the summer of 1959, the new pool opened, much to the delight of the town's hot and bored children.

The city provided swimming lessons to people in a wide range of ages, from young children to adults. The cost of the lessons was reasonable, and the instructors were capable.

When we first arrived in Winterset in 1957, my family had only one car that my father drove to work. Thus, Mom had no way to transport me to the pool. By the summer of 1960, Kay, now over three years old, was better able to be pulled in our Red Flyer wagon to the pool. Thus, I began lessons in June when I was seven and a half years old.

Early morning that first day, Mom, Kay, and I began our walk to the pool. We could take various routes, which we did over time to alter the scenic vistas on the mile-long walk. The most direct route, however, took us south on North Second Street for four blocks, where we turned right at the First Baptist Church. Then we traveled on Jefferson Street for about eleven blocks.

Our route took us past North Ward Elementary School and the pool hall, liquor store, and Northside Café. We passed the Farmers & Merchants State Bank, Mills' Chevrolet dealership, and the lumberyard. At that point, we were across the street from the local post office.

We continued into the more affluent section of Winterset. The houses were much larger, often being at least two stories high, sometimes three. The houses had roomy yards with many blooming flowers. Some even had iron fences edging their outer walks. Our trips through that area were cooler. The overhanging limbs of the hard maple trees gently touched each other in the middle of the street.

At Eighth Avenue, we reached an older section of Winterset. The houses were still large on big lots but lacked the professional landscaping that houses along Court and Jefferson Streets had. We had reached the area considered to be the edge of town. About three blocks further, the swimming pool sat by itself on the eastern edge of a cornfield.

As we approached the one-way drive that circled the pool, our legs were beginning to ache. The trip had been a long walk from home, and we were not yet used to such a journey. By the time we reached the pool, we'd all had our morning's exercise.

The pool building was constructed from tan-colored cement blocks. At the front entrance, we registered for my swimming lessons. The youngest children were scheduled to begin their swimming classes at nine o'clock in the morning. The sessions were scheduled for three days a week for six weeks.

Upon arriving, the boys turned right and the girls turned left into the appropriate changing and shower rooms. The rooms had no roof, being open to the elements in all types of weather.

I had carried my new swimming suit with me. That was the first time I had ever changed clothes in a public setting, for there were no private changing rooms. I quickly slipped out of my shorts and into my suit.

When registering, I had been told that all persons using the pool had to have a shower first before entering the pool water. I climbed into the shower area and pulled the silver chain to release the shower's water.

At that point, I discovered why I was no longer enthusiastic about taking swimming lessons. In Iowa in early June, the nights are often quite cool, going down into the fifties or sixties. I discovered when I pulled the shower chain how cold the water also was in the early morning.

The nearly frigid fluid gushed out the shower nozzle and onto my hair, swimsuit, and exposed skin. In the open shower, the sun shone brightly overhead, but it provided no heat that early in the day. The outside air was around seventy degrees.

My skin immediately erupted into goosebumps.

From that point on until the swimming lesson concluded and I had again dressed in my shorts, I continued to shiver.

Parents and other relatives were not allowed in the swimming area during the children's lessons. They had to remain outside the surrounding eight-foot high fence. Mom took Kay's hand and retreated through the entryway. I wrapped my towel around my shaking shoulders and headed out the doorway to the pool.

After being directed to the appropriate beginners' group, I stood on the cold concrete at the edge of the water. The female instructor was friendly and explained the rules of using the pool. "You are not to run, push other children, act rowdy, or in any other way totally embarrass your proud parents," who would be summoned if we acted unruly.

I remember little of that first day. My shivering body made it difficult to concentrate. In the early Iowa morning, just enough breeze blew through my wet hair and suit to thoroughly chill my bones.

When the instructor first had us jump in the water, my worst fears were confirmed. The temperature of the water was even colder than the outside air. My teeth began to chatter from the total immersion. Even after we had begun our first movements in the pool, my body could not warm up.

Finally, the forty-five-minute class was over. All the students stretched the rule about not running in the pool area. We managed to speed walk around the north end of the pool and into the showers on the east side. We all set records for how fast we could rinse off the pool's chlorine, again in the cold shower water, and dress in our street clothes.

After a mile's walk to the pool and a long swimming lesson, I had to walk back home with Mom and Kay. The heat of the rising morning sun warmed the outdoor air. By the time we reached home, I felt starved, yet ready to collapse on the nearest horizontal piece of furniture.

I never got used to the cold pool water in the early mornings. As I grew older, making it all the way to intermediate swimmers' class, my swimming lessons were scheduled later in the morning. By eleven o'clock, the temperature of the outside air and the water temperature were more equal and bearable. By the second week of July when swimming lessons concluded, even the youngest children were comfortable in the pool.

The general public could swim from one until four o'clock in the afternoon and from seven until nine in the evening. Sometimes on the days I did not have lessons, Mom felt it was important for me to have some practice time.

Thus, we trekked the long distance back to the pool in the afternoon's heat. I could swim alone in the four-foot end under the watchful eyes of two lifeguards. Mom took Kay to the wading pool for toddlers at the northeast corner of the pool compound. The wading pool had a separate gated entrance so young children could not wander out of the area and tumble into the main pool's deeper waters.

When Kay and I were old enough, we were finally allowed to make the pool journey by ourselves. We often debated whether or not the long walk to the pool in the early afternoon heat and seemingly longer walk home in the afternoon's broiling sun were worth the three hours of cool swimming pleasure.

Learning to swim was considered important safety training even in landlocked Iowa. Parents were willing to spend precious dollars to have their children learn to swim. I understood and valued that potential life-saving skill. I could never figure out, however, why the youngest children had to take their lessons at the coldest time of the morning.

RELATIVES AND OTHER PEOPLE

To a child under ten, the world is a jumble of people who must be sorted into categories. Aunts and uncles, first cousins, second cousins, and cousins beyond that all expect to be called relatives.

People who are called "aunt" or "uncle" so-and-so also appear and are really grandaunts or granduncles. They are the sisters and brothers of one's grandparents.

Then some people a child is supposed to call "aunt" or "uncle" aren't really blood relatives at all. This is just an honorary title for a special family friend.

In the latter category was Aunt Jenny. I barely understood how Aunt Jenny appeared in my life.

To children, parents don't have past lives. The lives of parents begin when they marry and have children. Time passes for a child from that point forward. Yet, somehow, grownups do have a life history that intrudes into the present in the oddest ways.

When a child asks about his or her parents' past lives, the child is often told not to ask questions. This merely leaves an air of mystery, which, of course, a child's curiosity requires be examined.

Such was the case with Aunt Jenny.

Aunt Jenny was a gentle soul who lived in Maryville, Missouri, and whose deeply wrinkled face made the cutest quilted patterns when she smiled at me. She always wore her long, multi-hued gray hair in a tight bun on the crest of her head. She had been a part of my life as long as I could remember.

I had figured out that Aunt Jenny wasn't really a

blood relative. At first, she was just a sweet old lady who our family visited every once in a while. Often on our infrequent weekend visits to Missouri, before the family headed back to Iowa, we stopped to say hello to Aunt Jenny.

As I grew, that began to seem odd. If Aunt Jenny was just a friend, why were the trips to see her so regular? We rarely visited other old friends of my mother as much. When I attempted to pose questions, Mom deftly dodged them.

Aunt Jenny's tiny house was filled with items I considered to be antiques. To Aunt Jenny, those household objects had been used all her life. She didn't consider herself old enough to have antiques, even though she was well past seventy.

She had an old Victrola, heavy wooden tables, and old vases. A glider rocking chair easily slid forward and backward, the first rocker of that type I had ever seen. Prominently displayed on a small table in the living room was an aging photograph of a young man in a World War II Army uniform.

As I studied his face, I realized I had seen it elsewhere in the house. The photograph hung on the yellowed wallpaper in the living room. A similar oval portrait sat on the bureau in Aunt Jenny's bedroom. No one mentioned Aunt Jenny having a son.

I finally guessed that the man in the photograph had died. I had a good sense of when grownups avoided my questions and when such questions shouldn't be asked at all. The mystery, however, was too good and had to be probed.

One day I summoned my courage and asked Mom and Aunt Jenny about the man. Silence filled the room for a moment too long. I recall the conversation went along the following lines.

"He was Aunt Jenny's son Ted," Mom told me.

I considered the statement and the extended pause after it, but I had gone too far to stop now. "Where is he?" I queried gently.

After a pause, Mom replied, "He died shortly after the war."

I looked from one face to the next. I suspected Mom knew that would not be the end of my quest. She had seen my penetrating gaze before.

I put off further questions for another day. I knew the grownups were hiding something. I knew it involved pain, and I also knew I had to know what the grownups were reluctant to discuss.

Every subsequent visit brought more tidbits of information. Whenever we arrived at Aunt Jenny's house, I sat quietly in the background. Aunt Jenny always gave Kay and me an entire candy bar apiece as a treat. We didn't have to share the candy bar like we did at home.

I took mine and found a strategic seat in the foyer corner, near the living room. Being exceptionally quiet, I listened to the conversations between Mom and Aunt Jenny. I knew eavesdropping wasn't permitted, but the situation had consumed my curiosity and wouldn't let go.

The two women talked of old times. Mom had lived near Aunt Jenny's family for years. They spoke of neighbors they knew, some living, most dead. They discussed Aunt Jenny's health and the high cost of groceries. They admired Aunt Jenny's huge Christmas cactus plant that bloomed from Thanksgiving until well after Christmas. Always a special bond existed between them that I sensed was more than one between old friends.

Finally, one day, I caught Mom at home at a vulnerable moment. I again asked about the young man and Aunt Jenny.

With a very living-in-the-past look in her eyes, Mom gazed over the clothesline toward the morning sun. She stared so long I began to wonder if she were hypnotized.

Mom slowly turned her head toward me. "She's too young, yet," must have been her first thought. "She can't understand life's complexities." In her heart, I'm sure, however, that she knew I was older than my years at times.

The story finally came out. Mom and Ted had grown up around Maryville and their families had known each other. Ted had been friends with one of her four brothers in their younger days. They had all teased the baby sister, my mother, who was too tall and slender for her own good.

Ted had still been there when Mom had eventually blossomed. Mom had a sharp mind and a level head on her shoulders. Ted was a strong, tall, good-looking farm boy. Their friendship turned into dreams of a future life on a farm of their own.

Then World War II began. Although young and able to claim an exemption for being needed to work the family farm, Ted had enlisted. Being a Missouri farm boy, he chose the Army where he could keep his feet on dry land.

Nobody in that part of Missouri paid much attention to world events. Nobody believed the war would last long anyway, but Ted was willing to add his part to the effort.

Off Ted went to the nearest training base, while Mom attended college to earn her teaching degree. Letters from the two romantics filled the mail sacks to and from his bases. A few times, Ted received a weekend pass and Mother picked him up at the Maryville train or bus station. Ted later served in England at an Army Air Corps station as a mechanic for B-17 bombers.

Finally, the war was over, and Ted returned stateside. Before he could be discharged one weekend, however, he said he wasn't feeling well. He had a stomachache.

Most farm folks like Ted figured they could take care of their family members themselves whenever they were ill. Children were always catching the sniffles, stomach flu was a fact of life each winter, and bronchitis often occurred in the damp, chilly spring. Country folks just didn't go see a doctor until they became extremely ill. Unfortunately, too many people waited until precisely that moment to rush to the doctor's office.

By early Monday morning, the telephone call had come. Ted's appendix had burst Sunday night. The doctors had not been able to stop the infection. Ted had died.

My mother's future wedding dreams disappeared. Aunt Jenny, Mom, her brothers, her mother, and all of Aunt Jenny's relatives buried Ted in the rich Missouri soil that had nurtured him all his life.

Ted had loved the land. He had tilled it since he had been old enough to walk, first in the family garden, then on the family acreage. Now he was returned to it.

A long pause followed while Mom and I thought

about two different worlds.

I realized then that Aunt Jenny might have become my grandmother under different circumstances. Only then I would not have been the same me because I would have had a different father.

I pondered that thought. I hadn't yet learned about genetics, but I knew a child looked like his or her parents.

Closing my eyes, I pictured the photograph of the young man in my mind. I looked at his smile. I liked it and the confident posture of his shoulders.

I began to sense all the variations of chance meetings, growing relationships, and love that combine, seemingly randomly, to create a life together for a couple. I considered the possible matching of my mother and Ted, two people who might have been my parents, but it was never meant to be.

I then thought about the two people who had become my parents. I marveled at life's mysteries.

FALL AND HALLOWEEN FRIGHTS

Fall in central Iowa brought chilly winds and colorful leaves. Hundreds of large hard maple trees lining my hometown's streets blazed with color.

On autumn weekends, parental duties included raking the leaves into piles. Adults saw that as a chore resulting in aching backs. We children saw an opportunity to play in those leaf mounds.

Ray and I loved fall. We selected our favorite colorful leaves and found places of honor for them in our bedrooms. We pressed some leaves between sheets of newspaper, but the colors always faded slightly after they dried.

Outside, we heaped the leaves into the largest pile possible. Then we ran leaping into the air, throwing ourselves on top of the piles.

After reshaping the pile, we raced full speed into them, headfirst, sending the leaves scattering in all directions. We emerged, spewing bits of broken leaves from our mouths and pulling them from our hair. Throughout the day, the musty aroma of decaying leaves clung to our clothes.

In the fall of 1960, an abundance of leaves meant we had to build a leaf fort. My front yard was transformed into a battle zone. We confiscated every leaf in the neighborhood to build the fort's walls as high as two pairs of young arms could reach. Then we defended our fort against all imagined invading enemies.

We guarded our fort by day, dreading the nights. Then higher parental authorities forced us to abandon our post for bed. Nights meant marauding enemies in the form of older neighborhood teenagers. They often destroyed our fort out of sheer orneriness, especially at Halloween.

In my room, the two west windows faced the front yard of the house. Sometimes they remained open at night so I could smell the wonderful drying leaves. I left the window blinds up slightly so I could watch our fort from my bed. I guarded it each night, at least until I fell asleep.

The location of my bedroom led to another Halloween-time scare. As an astute almost-nine-year-old, I understood that Halloween was make-believe. No werewolves or vampires existed, only people dressed in costumes. The darkness, however, brought the shadows of creatures that looked real to me.

Diagonally across the street from my house stood the only streetlight at my end of the block. The streetlight had a bulb of dubious wattage. The bulb produced enough light by which to see to walk, but not enough to distinguish objects well.

As Halloween approached, our fort often blew apart in the gusty evening winds. The friendly leaves of daytime became the shuffling mystery noises of night.

The streetlight shone through the maple trees lining the curb outside my window. Eerie shadows were cast into my bedroom. Gnarly fingers on the bony hands of monster arms danced around the walls and onto the ceiling.

As the winds blew, the many arms and fingers entwined, appearing to shake hands or fight with one another. They reached up in horror or sagged to the floor in despair. In my imagination, the sounds of creaking tree limbs and rustling leaves became footsteps outside my window.

I felt trapped between reality and my imagination. I thought bogey men did not exist, but in my room was proof that opinion might be wrong. The shadow fingers reached for me in the darkness. The moans of their owners assailed my ears.

I sometimes thought that, perhaps, spirits of dead people did haunt the earth. Perhaps the grownups were wrong. After all, adults had been proven to be in error about babies being brought by storks.

Huddling under the covers did not alleviate my fright. Beneath the quilts was only total darkness, just like under the bed. A smart child never let her hand hang over the edge of the bed. One never knew what lurked in the shadows underneath.

Eventually, I peeked out to see if the dancing devils had disappeared. They had not.

Too proud to call for help, I stared hypnotically at the demons prancing around my bedroom. I watched as they twisted, departed, shifted, shook, and clawed at the bedroom walls. While they never actually touched me, I felt they could if they became angry.

I lay quietly, not moving a muscle, frozen in time and space. I lay watching, watching, until I no longer saw them. Finally, I fell asleep.

Then morning arrived. I was glad the shadow demons proved too cowardly to appear in the daylight. They continued to wait for me each night, however, especially as Halloween approached.

THE WORLD TURNS TO ICE

Winter often brought gloriously snowy landscapes to Iowa. In mid-February 1961 when I was eight years old, however, Winterset had its most destructive ice storm in history.

Mom taught fourth grade at North Ward Elementary School, one block south of our house. After school, Kay and I stayed with Mrs. Albers until Mother finished her workday. Mrs. Albers lived on the corner across the street from the school.

One noon, heavy snow began to fall. By late afternoon, the ground was already white, with more snow cascading down like a white flakey waterfall.

Mom often worked grading papers after school ended. On that day, she later told me how she looked out the window and knew she'd better leave soon. She gathered her paperwork to take with her and left the school into a full snowstorm.

The snow was already knee deep and visibility down to less than two blocks. Mom decided to go home first before she picked up us girls.

Carrying her schoolwork and purse, Mom struggled through the snowdrifts. Reaching the house, she grabbed a large, metal snow shovel and began shoveling a one-block path back down the sidewalk to Mrs. Albers's house.

Each snowfall has its own characteristics. The Eskimos have over a dozen words for different kinds of snow. On that day, the snow was loaded with moisture as it fell. Such snow accumulates fast and heavily weighs down a shovel when trying to remove it.

Mom had worked a long day, but she was determined to bring her daughters home before total darkness arrived. She shoveled a narrow path, throwing scoopfuls downwind of the bitter breeze. Her muscles ached by the time she reached Mrs. Albers.

The usual pleasantries had to be skipped. Mrs. Albers quickly bundled Kay and me in our winter attire, while Mom caught her breath. The snow continued piling up, but delays only meant further trouble returning home.

With Mom leading the way, Kay and I trailed behind. Now heading north, Mom had to face the bitter winter wind as she again shoveled a small path homeward. The path she had first made to Mrs. Albers' house had nearly filled with new snow.

As fast as Mom shoveled, the wind blew snow back onto the path. With our short legs, we tried to stay upright on the white, uneven trail, with wind gusts knocking us about at will.

How exhausted Mom must have been by the time she spied our house. Day had already passed into the early darkness of the winter's evening. The dim streetlight from the north end of the block provided little illumination during a snowstorm.

After a few final scoopfuls, Mom pulled us up the front steps and onto the south porch, out of the wind. There we paused.

Covered head to toe in snowy white, we all looked like abominable snowwomen in our thick winter coats, hats, scarves, boots, and mittens. We brushed snow off each other's clothing as best as we could with cold-stiffened hands. Then we each shook like water-soaked dogs to remove more of the clinging whiteness.

After we had shaken loose most of the snowflakes, we dashed into the warmth of the house. We pulled off our mittens and quickly blew on our cold fingers. When some feeling returned to our hands, we fumbled with coat buttons and wet neck scarves. Mother brought towels to dry our faces where snowflakes had thawed, wetting on our eyelashes and hair.

The snow fell most of the night. After midnight, however, the real winter storm arrived.

A furious ice storm began with pleasant tinkles of miniature ice drops pinging against the windowpanes. Then the pinging became more insistent. Finally, I could not see out the windowpanes, because the drops had formed ice sheets. The view from an ice-covered window made the world look like the shapes in a carnival house of mirrors; everything was distorted and misshapen.

The morning after the ice storm was eerily quiet. Little or no breeze disturbed the landscape. Even the animals stayed in their burrows.

On that day, the worst situation occurred. A steady wind rose, bringing further danger. As the wind blew through the ice-laden tree limbs, a surreal creaking began. The limbs in the trees moaned and groaned like stairsteps in an old haunted house. The thin tree limbs at the ends of the branches formed icy fingers that clinked together. They broke off from the weight of the ice, like dried bones dropping from a cold weathered skeleton.

Everything outside wore over a half-inch thick coating of ice. The tree limbs could no longer stand the added weight, combined with the steady wind. They began to break.

All over the neighborhood, breaking tree limbs crashed to the ground and onto anything beneath them. Cars without garages became their first targets. Even Ray's cherry tree suffered from the onslaught. Until the wind stopped, we were not allowed to play outside for fear a tree limb might hurtle down upon our heads.

In our backyard, one of the two cedar trees that supported our swing became a storm victim. The tree had two main branches forming a "V." One large branch broke off, luckily dropping east onto the yard and away from the house. The branch lay on the icy snow like a fallen soldier on a bitterly cold battlefield.

As the icy destruction continued, the next fatalities became telephone and electrical lines. In the early 1960s, most utility cables were above ground, making them easy targets for any winter storm. That day's weather produced a serious ice storm, and the aftermath was becoming costly.

Dad had been working out of town the day the snowstorm began. By evening, snow buried the two-lane highways too deeply for him to return home safely. A family in Patterson, a small town twelve miles east of Winterset, welcomed him.

In the Midwest, sudden snowstorms often brought out the warm hospitality of the region's people. Total strangers were welcomed into homes where they were fed, housed, and entertained until the highway maintenance crews cleared the roads. Families who opened their homes never accepted offers of payment from their visitors. Those hosts felt they were extending a small favor in advance, for they might be the ones in need during the next blizzard.

By morning, Mom, Kay, and I awoke to a cold house. Our furnace burned coal, but it required an electric fan to blow the heat from the basement air ducts and throughout the house. With the electrical wires down, the fan had no power.

We reluctantly inched out of our warm beds. Handmade family quilts covered us all night, so winter's cold never reached us while we slept. When our warm toes touched the cold hardwood floors, however, we glanced longingly at those thick covers.

We dressed rapidly. The cold house meant we donned our warmest socks, slacks, boots, long-sleeved shirts and sweaters, and winter coats. We even donned our winter hats and gloves. The cold of an unheated house managed to penetrate our bones after just a few hours.

Our family was more fortunate than many in Winterset. We had a gas cooking stove, so Mom kept us supplied with hot food for the next three days that we spent without electricity.

We girls had often envied Ray for his nicer material possessions, but his family had to abandon their all-electric house next door. With no way to heat their house or to prepare warm food, hypothermia could have become a serious threat. For once, having the latest technology proved a life-threatening hindrance.

Walking carefully, Ray's family inched their way slowly out of their house and across the icy streets, dodging downed tree limbs. They managed to reach Ray's grandmother's house a block away. They remained there until electric power returned. Ray's grandmother had a gas cooking stove and a wood-burning fireplace.

Tommy Thompson's dump truck normally appeared regularly at our house all winter. We would watch the truck pull to a stop along the street north of our house. Backing over the curb, the truck eased across the frozen yard until it neared the north side of the house.

Thompson's hired man opened the coal chute doors into our basement, pulled out the truck's slide, and raised the truck bed enough for the coal chunks to begin sliding downhill. He guided the coal toward the slide, continuing to empty the truck until the coal bin in the basement was full. Then he drove the truck away, until called to return again in a week or two.

With my father stranded by the storm, the furnace became my mother's responsibility. Although we had no electric power to operate the fans, the furnace continued to burn coal. Her job was to fill the coal hopper attached to the furnace. The hopper was a metal box about four feet square. Coal chunks were stored there, until the auger pulled the coal into the furnace fire.

Mother managed to load a few coal chunks onto a shovel and into the hopper. She made many trips back and forth from the coal bin to the furnace until the hopper was full. On that day, the auger was useless due to the lack of electricity. By keeping the hopper full, she could reach for coal chunks and toss them into the furnace after she opened its small door.

Upstairs, soft wisps of warm air rose gently from the floor airduct vents. When we really needed to feel heat, my sister and I stood over the metal decorative vents and almost felt a slight warmth rising like a whisper from the furnace.

As the days progressed, we tried to keep busy in order to stay warm. We played games, did housework, and watched the tree limbs crash to the ground.

The kitchen had two doors, one to the living room and one to the bathroom. Mom closed both doors to retain whatever heat remained from cooking our meals. Every few hours, she turned on the gas oven, opened the oven door, and heated the kitchen's air to a livable degree of warmth. The oven could not be used as a heating source for any length of time since the procedure could result in carbon monoxide poisoning. For as long as we could, we stayed in the heated kitchen.

For three days, we lived in an icy world. Of course, we played outside after the wind died down and the tree limbs stopped falling. We slid on the frozen ground as if we were wearing ice skates. We dragged out our sled and took turns trying to pull each other. With no traction, however, the one pulling could never build up any momentum, so the sled failed to travel very fast or any great distance.

Being without electricity was the closest we children ever came to our grandparents' pioneer days. Months after the ice storm, when our elders would begin, "I remember when I was a boy...," we were more able to understand what they meant.

Living through Iowa winters teaches people to be resourceful and logical in a dangerous situation. A way could always be found to handle a crisis, if only a girl used her head. I learned that among the best ways to use my head during an ice storm was to wear a hat in our unheated house.

SUMMER SAILBOAT

Iowa summers always appeared with brilliant emerald-colored grass as soft as baby's skin. The softness of Winterset grass proved irresistible to me. I discarded my shoes as soon as the weather warmed and avoided donning them whenever possible the rest of the summer.

In the summer of 1961, I was eight years old. On one beautiful day, the hard maple trees were loaded with leaves fluttering like large green flags that waved whenever a breeze passed through them. While the robins chirped merrily overhead, I gazed at the tranquil scene, searching for something to do.

After a while, Ray, or the more formal Raymond as his mother called him, sauntered out his back door. I decided that Ray might know some game to play. Although I was usually the more assertive one, on that day my mind felt dull and unimaginative.

Ray's bored expression soon pointed out that he also was having a bland day. The two of us retired to Ray's cherry tree in his backyard to meditate on the situation.

The morning dragged by as we sat and dangled our legs from a tree branch. Occasionally we dropped green cherries on some unsuspecting ant scurrying along the ground beneath us. That was the kind of morning when our imaginations proved blank and nothing unusual happened in the quiet neighborhood.

At last, Ray's father came home for lunch. Ray's mother popped her head out the door and called Raymond inside to eat. I took a parachute leap from the tree and vanished into my house for my noon meal. In a small town, everyone ate meals at the same time, right after the noon fire department whistle blew. The meal schedule was as regular as the sunrise and sunset.

Afternoon brought a turn of events. Ray's father said that his family planned to buy a new wooden picnic table. He gave Ray and me permission to demolish the old one.

For the first time in my life, I thought about the differences that having money could make. Ray was considered to be the rich boy in our middle-class neighborhood; his father was a real estate agent. I was one of the less rich children.

Ray was lucky. How many children were allowed to tear up a perfectly good picnic table just because it had a few warped boards?

Ray's dad loaned us some tools, and that afternoon we began a major demolition job under the sycamore tree in Ray's backyard. With carefully placed knocks, we youngsters hammered the undersides of the old slats until the nails lifted out from the connecting boards. After pulling out all visible nails, bending a few in the process, we stacked the lumber in neat piles on the grass.

By evening the old picnic table had been dismantled. We surveyed our work with pride. The day had been a great one for demolition work.

The next morning, Ray's father informed us that we had to move the lumber because the grass under the pile was turning a pale yellow. That posed the problem of what to do with all those boards. For two landlubbers from Iowa, the most obvious solution was to build a boat.

Over the next two days, we inexperienced carpenters hammered and sawed, building a boat as well-constructed as a six- and an eight-year-old normally could build. I did most of the hammering because I could hit the nails without bending them. Ray did the sawing because his father owned the saw.

Our vessel turned out shaped like a rowboat, with two cross boards for seats. From somewhere, we procured a miniature steamboat-style steering wheel and nailed it to a vertical board in the middle of the boat.

Ray and I decided not to put a bottom in the boat because the cool grass felt good on our bare feet. Besides, we ran out of lumber before we could even think of adding a hull.

On the day of completion, a christening party was held, celebrated with Kool-Aid and cookies. The flaking, faded, barn-red paint of the warped picnic table boards clashed with the emerald green of the grass. To us two proud sailors, however, it was the best boat that ever sailed the bounding main.

Ray and I both decided to be captains of the boat so we would not have to fight over who would give or take orders. Since Ray had a light blue captain's hat with an anchor on it, he steered the boat most of the time. Usually my ideas, however, took precedence for which places to explore.

For nearly two weeks, we mariners dutifully moved our boat to a new spot each morning. The grass always turned yellow under the boat after it had set in one place for an entire day. Then, we made sail for distant ports.

One day, we attacked the pirate's fort in the nearby sandbox. The next day we sailed under the storm clouds caused by the shadow of the cherry tree. We freed the imaginary princess held in the enemy fortress in the hedgerow by pretending to bombard the fort into little pieces.

We mapped every island in the Pacific. We thoroughly searched secret coves in the Caribbean for hidden treasure. Through fierce storms and balmy breezes, we sailors floated around the globe.

Each morning as we relocated our boat, we plotted the day's course through new waters. Each evening, we moored in the nearest friendly harbor to await the morning's tide.

Through our imaginations, the entire world was ours. As clearly as we could see the cherry tree and Ray's house, we could envision all the places our small boat sailed. Like all children, Ray and I could turn reality into fantasy from breakfast to lunch, and from lunch to supper.

Living in a small town only enhanced our curiosity about the world around us. As children, we eventually lost interest in the boat. As adults, we sailed our separate ways into life.

The memory of our adventure lingers. I still recall the summer afternoon we built a boat and sailed around the world.

TRIPS TO TOWN

In the early 1960s, one advantage my paternal grandparents had over my parents was virtually un-limited free time. Once Grandpa Lyle retired, he and Grandma Mary puttered in their garden, did house-cleaning, and visited friends. Grandpa Lyle continued to raise a few head of cattle. They loved to have us grandchildren come to visit.

Beginning around age eight in 1961, I occasionally spent the weekend or a few days in the summer at my grandparents' farm outside Macksburg. Being there provided a calmness in my life, a sense of timelessness with little need to hurry. My grandparents had their daily routine, and I blended into it.

Around the time I was born, Grandma Mary had been diagnosed with rheumatoid arthritis. As long as I could remember, she could only move by slowly shuf-fling her feet around the house. Her fingers, which had once been extremely slender and delicate, now had knots at every joint from the effects of the arthritis. She never complained and still carried out her household activities. Only when she needed to lift anything heavy or delicate did she ask for assistance from Grandpa and me.

My grandparents began each day shortly after day-light, continuing the habits of early rising that most farm families acquired. Grandma slowly dressed and started to prepare breakfast. Grandpa set the table and brought items to within Grandma's reach.

After breakfast, we did the dishes. I always hated

doing dishes by hand, but I was expected to help, so I did. With three of us, the few dirty dishes were soon clean and returned to the cupboards.

Then Grandma watered her African violets sitting on the north windowsill and completed other housekeeping tasks. She still tried to dust and make the beds. Every activity took her a long time to finish, but she had been told by the doctors that she should keep moving. If she ever stopped doing as much physical activity as she could, she knew the arthritis would completely lock her joints and she would never be able to move them. As long as I knew her, she rarely took any medication for her condition.

Grandpa proceeded outdoors. He fed his beloved dog Lassie, a black-and-white collie. Lassie was totally devoted to Grandpa, and he returned the feelings.

When I was small, Grandma and Grandpa still had about fifty laying hens in the large chicken coop just north of the house. Grandpa carefully gathered the eggs and carried them into the house in a gray metal bucket. Grandma picked up each egg and, using an old sturdy sock, cleaned off any straw or dirt on the eggshells. Then the eggs were placed in one-foot square cartons with cardboard separation layers and stored in the cool cellar. The man who drove the egg truck came by every couple of days to collect them.

Sometimes Grandpa and I hoed in their small garden. Other times we just walked around the central area between the house, old barn, machinery sheds, and corn cribs.

Then it was time to climb into his white Rambler sedan and drive north through the gate into the pasture. The pasture contained the sledding hill we used in winter. That area also was home to his Angus cattle and the Stratton gas pump that brought up the well water for his thirsty herd.

The pump and large galvanized water tank sat at the bottom of the sledding hill. Grandpa had to check each day to see if the tank contained enough water to satisfy the cattle's thirst until the next morning.

We slowly drove downhill to the tank and turned on the pump if the water level was low. While we waited for the tank to fill, Grandpa counted the cows to see that all were present and healthy. In summer, the cows ate pasture grass. In winter, Grandpa provided them hay.

I ran my hands through the well water as it spewed from the spout. I was always amazed at how cold the water was. Sometimes I splashed some on Grandpa, who acted totally surprised.

Next, we drove back to the house. Grandpa parked his Rambler at the end of the sidewalk leading to the house's side door.

We checked with Grandma. If Grandma needed any groceries or other supplies, she made a list. She knew Grandpa might forget an item if she just told him. Men proved forgetful when they started talking with their friends. Grandpa and I washed our hands, combed our hair, and prepared for Grandpa's almost daily trip to town.

Grandpa's farm lay one-half mile east and one mile north of Macksburg. Six days a week, after chores were done, Grandpa drove to town.

Grandpa kept an old braided rug on the backseat. With a short yell, Grandpa called Lassie. She promptly appeared, wagging her tail furiously, eager for the daily ride.

Lassie leaped onto the backseat as soon as Grandpa opened the door. She remained there during our visit to town. Lassie loved to place her nose outside the window and overload her senses with all the interesting smells.

I climbed in the front seat. In those days, cars did not have seatbelts. I rolled down the window to smell the countryside as we drove along. Often, I held my hand outside the car window in the airstream, with the currents raising and lowering my hand like an airplane.

Because of Grandpa's poor eyesight from the effects of glaucoma, he tended to drive quite slowly. He used the excuse that he enjoyed watching what the neighboring farmers had done to their farms and seeing how much the crops had grown. I did not mind the slow trip; it just made the journey last longer.

When we first entered the eastern limits of Macksburg, we passed the house of Grandpa's cousin Earl Whitworth and his wife Luella. Sometimes they were working in the yard or sitting on the front porch, so we waved. Macksburg was so small, with a population of around 225 people, that my arrival at Grandpa's farm was quickly noted.

After driving one block farther, Grandpa pulled to a stop alongside the U.S. Post Office building. The tiny wooden structure of, perhaps, fifteen feet square was an officially designated Post Office. Fern, the postmistress, was a distant cousin of ours. I had many distant cousins in Macksburg, where my ancestors had first arrived in 1870 and married into other local families in the small farming community.

Grandpa gathered the mail from his box, and Fern always commented on how much I had grown since she had last seen me. Grandpa beamed with pride as if he had personally made me grow. I almost blushed from the unaccustomed attention.

We returned to the car and drove one block farther to Holiday's Grocery Store, the only one in Macksburg. Grandpa ambled up the sidewalk, waving to any old friends sitting on the wooden porch benches outside the grocery.

East of the grocery store was Earl Whitworth's barber shop. Beyond that was the veterinarian's office, and sometimes the vet saw us and waved.

Inside the grocery store, everyone knew Grandpa. Greetings were exchanged, and the conversations began. I was properly acknowledged and mumbled something in return. Then I looked around the grocery store as something to do while Grandpa talked.

Holiday's Grocery Store always reminded me of mercantile shops that I had seen in old western cowboy photographs. Shelving was everywhere, all taller than I was. A variety of canned and bottled food products were available, the staples that farming families ate. The floor was constructed of wooden slats worn smooth from years of farm boots treading them. They tended to creak when I walked around the aisles.

Finally, Grandpa ended his conversations. Then he took his time selecting the grocery items from Grandma's list. He carried them to the front checkout counter and laid them on the vinyl countertop.

Next, Grandpa looked at me and said, "I reckon you ought to have some ice cream." I nodded my head, half seriously, and replied, "I reckon I could." Then he nodded his head in the direction of the refrigerated case.

Suppressing my eagerness, I walked as casually as Grandpa did over to the case. The ice cream freezer was made of white, enamel-coated metal. The case stood about three feet high and four feet wide, with a flat top containing two sliding glass doors. I could just see over the top of the case to study the potential selections inside.

Options included Eskimo Pies, orange sherbet push-up pops, Drumsticks, and Twin Pops. At home in Winterset, my family only bought half gallons of ice cream, and then only when they were on sale. We rarely bought individual ice cream treats, deeming them too expensive for the quantity of ice cream received.

Grandpa, however, saw the treat as his special gift to me each time we went to town. I gave my choice careful consideration. As with most children, I wanted to select one of each, but I knew that was considered frivolous. Whatever my taste buds preferred that morning, I followed their choice.

Sliding back one door, I reached into the frosty coldness and pulled out an individual ice cream item. Grandpa nodded at the grocery store owner who added the cost of my treat to the small grocery ticket. Grandpa paid and we sauntered out the door, climbing back into his Rambler.

Sometimes, Grandpa bought an ice cream for himself, too. We ate in companionable silence as he made a U-turn and drove slowly back toward his farm.

That was our time of day to be alone. We rarely had any deep or insightful conversations. We were just two souls who enjoyed ice cream and each other's company. That was enough.

CHERRY TREE DARES

In the entire neighborhood, only Raymond's cherry tree provided climbing access for a pair of brave children. The cherry tree stood about twenty feet tall on Ray's side of the boundary sidewalk separating our backyards.

Each year the tree produced a bumper crop of tart red cherries. The berries resulted in cherry pies, but that was not why we valued the tree. Its worth was measured in climbing height and its ability to inspire supposedly life-threatening dares in the summer of 1961.

Our dares fell into three categories: closed eyes, climbing height, and touch the wire. The categories designated the extent of the imagined danger involved.

The cherry tree had one limb about four inches thick, the one required for the closed eyes dare. The limb grew horizontally about four feet off the ground, pointing south.

For the first dare, each of us took turns squatting on the horizontal limb, balancing as well as possible. The darer stood on the ground before the limb to watch for cheating. The daree was required to close his or her eyes, jump off the limb, and keep both eyes closed all the way to the ground. Whoever opened his or her eyes on the way to landing on the ground lost the dare.

That was rated as a minimum danger dare. Connecting with the ground with one's eyes closed always resulted in a serious tingling in the feet and ankles. We learned that, without one's eyes alerting the brain to prepare for impact, landing was very jarring to the body. A minor sprained ankle sometimes resulted.

The second level dare consisted of the highest climb. Cherry trees have rather thin limbs, at best. The higher we climbed, the thinner the branches become. By the time either of us reached the uppermost branches, the limbs were bending severely and threatening to break.

Of course, the dare required we climb onto horizontal branches, which flexed even more than vertical ones. That added to our sense of danger. The loser was the one who chickened out before the branch broke. The winner climbed the highest, stayed the longest, but did not come crashing to the ground.

Ray and I competed in the most dangerous dare—touch the wire—only on an extremely competitive day. That dare required serious life and death danger, at least in the minds of a six-year-old and an eight-year-old. Neither of us, however, could possibly back away once dared.

Through the uppermost branches of the cherry tree passed a black cable. Other neighborhood children speculated that the cable was merely a telephone line.

Ray and I discounted that opinion. We had faith the cable carried an electrical voltage capable of frying any child to the appearance of blackened toast.

With all the solemnity the occasion required, Ray and I faced the cherry tree. For the imagined life and death dare, both of us had to climb the tree at the same time.

We grasped the four-foot branch and swung our legs over the limb. Pulling ourselves onto the limb, we then positioned our bodies so the main vertical tree trunk divided us.

Slowly we began our climb. Carefully, we placed each foot on ascending limbs, pulling ourselves up by skinny arms. As we both climbed, our weight pulled on the thinning branches. The wind added to our swaying, which worsened as we neared the top.

Overhead stretched "The Wire." Finally, we were both within arm's length of our nemesis. We paused to catch our breath. Eyeing each other, we tried to gauge the other's determination to carry through with the ultimate dare.

Deciding that neither was going to chicken out, we inched our arms upward. Counting one...two...three, we were both supposed to grasp the assumed electrical line at the same time. The loser was the person who did not have the courage to touch the cable.

We had a logical explanation for why neither of us ever died from that dare. In our scientific view, we believed that electrical current passed through wires in pulses. By the luck of Russian roulette, Ray and I always managed to grasp the wire at the precise moment after one electrical pulse had just passed and before the next pulse surged down the wire.

The ultimate dare required only that we touch the cable. The dare didn't say anything about how long we had to hold onto it. Thus, our touch, logically, was only a millisecond long.

We were daredevils, after all, not crazy. In our minds, a longer hold meant certain death. Neither of us could ever have explained to the other's mother how important winning the ultimate dare was, even if it might have resulted in her offspring's death.

Our ultimate dare never involved any actual danger, since the cable, truly, was a telephone line. The implied life and death threat, however, was real to us at the time.

We daredevils later grew to love the heart-stopping thrill of carnival rides seemingly spinning beyond control to the brink of death. The lure of an adrenaline rush can be very addictive, lasting into adulthood in the form of parachute jumping, rock climbing, or trying to raise daredevil children. Such thrills can be formed in childhood by cherry tree dares.

ALLGEYER'S GROCERY STORE

Walking alone to Allgeyer's Grocery Store at age eight and a half in the summer of 1961 proved I was growing up. It also increased the wanderlust I had always possessed.

My first steps beyond the neighborhood boundaries my parents had established for me became my third major escape alone to the freedom of the outside world, after prior escapes at ages one and a half and three. For the trip to Allgeyer's, however, I actually had my parents' permission.

My parents had told me about my two unauthorized escapes to freedom beyond their control. At nine months of age, I had begun to walk. That was the day my mother's gray hairs first began to appear.

Evidently, I believed feet were for walking, at a minimum, and for running when my coordination improved. I intended to use my two appendages to their full extent. From the time I was born until I was almost two, our family of three lived in a small house on my grandfather's farm. One day when I was about one and a half years old, Mom looked up to find me gone from our unfenced front yard. She frantically began searching for me. She finally found me in a dangerous situation, at least from her viewpoint.

I had walked across the yard, across the driveway, and under a fence. I was happily strolling among large Angus cattle in the muddy feedlot near the barn.

Each cow weighed around 1,000 pounds. Mom immediately panicked, mentally picturing me squashed under the large bovine hooves. She promptly opened the gate, picked me up, and carried me be back to the house. That was probably the day I discovered I loved animals, for I was having a great time exploring.

My second escape came at age three. My parents had moved to a two-bedroom, two-story, rented house in Macksburg. Again, one day, Mom looked up to find that I had disappeared from the yard.

Macksburg had a population of just under 225 people. The town sat on flat land and had been platted into perfect squares. Everyone knew everyone else, including all their children. Eventually, one citizen looked out her window, saw me wandering down the sidewalk, and betrayed me by telephoning Mom.

My exploration of the outside world quickly ceased as soon as Mom arrived. I have been told I managed to reach a distance of two blocks from home before my recapture.

I was eight years old when my parents first officially allowed me to walk alone to Allgeyer's. The mom-and-pop grocery store at 420 Buchanan Street was located two and a half blocks east of our house in Winterset.

Mr. and Mrs. Allgeyer were a couple in their fifties. They had owned the neighborhood grocery store that bore their name since 1953. The store was open six days a week, from seven in the morning until six in the evening.

The grocery store was housed in a one-story building with a lower half of red brick and an upper portion painted a shade of aqua. Plate glass front windows and a glass front door allowed passersby to see inside.

Although the store's inventory was small, it provided all the staples a family could need. My family, however, only shopped there occasionally, because the prices were somewhat higher than the United Food Store where we usually shopped.

One day, Mom decided I was old enough to begin running errands for her. She allowed me to travel alone to Allgeyer's but first gave me a complete set of instructions. I was to place the money in my pocket and not lose it. I was to stay on the sidewalk that led directly to the store, with no side detours allowed. I was to watch for stray dogs and not pet them. I was to look both ways when I reached the one and only intersection of Buchanan and Fourth Streets that I had to cross.

I was told to buy only what was on the list my mother gave me. The Allgeyers would give me change from the five-dollar bill. To my surprise, I was given permission to spend two pennies on candy of my choice as a reward for running the shopping errand.

My pride at being allowed to make the journey almost matched my excitement at the prospect of the freedom to travel beyond Mom's eyesight. To reach Allgeyer's, I exited our back door and walked diagonally northeast across our backyard. At the corner of our neighbor's, the Bentons, driveway, I headed east on the sidewalk along Buchanan Street.

I took my time as I proceeded past the O'Malleys' house, then the houses of two unknown owners. I was so excited and busy looking around that I wandered back and forth from one edge of the sidewalk to the other. Although I had walked the route before with Mom and Kay, the pathway seemed entirely new when I could explore the sights at my own pace.

Finally, I reached the intersection of Buchanan and Fourth. I managed to focus my wandering attention to face the important task of safely crossing the street. I knew that if I were run over on my first trip to Allgeyer's, my future chances to escape from my own backyard would be greatly diminished. My parents would probably think I not was grown up enough to handle the responsibility, so I decided to obey Mom's directive to look both ways for cars.

Our neighborhood consisted of middle- to lower-middle class working people. The traffic count might reach twenty cars a day in each direction. Thus, my safety in crossing the street at mid-morning was a fairly minor concern at any time of year, but I paid attention anyway.

The scariest part of the trip was walking by the first house on the next block. The house was quite small, with trash and odd items like an old washing machine littering the unmown yard. Obviously, the owner, or more probably a renter, did not care about appearances. I had always felt uncomfortable walking near the house, and I quickened my pace to hurry beyond its sight.

Finally, after passing one tall pine tree, I reached Allgeyer's located in the middle of the block. I paused to look up at the name painted on the sign above the windows. How marvelous it must be, I reasoned, to own a business and have one's own name emblazoned above the door for everyone to admire.

I climbed the steps to the front door. Although tall for my age, I still had to reach up to the handle. I struggled to pull open the heavy front door. Then I arrived inside, all alone, with the responsibility of purchasing the items on the short grocery list.

I knew where the eggs and the half gallons of Anderson Erickson Dairy whole milk in waxed paper cartons were located and soon completed my shopping. I could then choose my candy reward.

In 1961, some candy could still be bought for one cent. Candy bars were a nickel and were of a decent size, not the tiny bars that now cost nearly two dollars.

I stared at the penny candy. My mouth began to water in anticipation. I surveyed the bite-sized Bit-O-Honeys, Super Bubble bubblegum, and Shari Smarties Super Sour Candy Rolls. An authentic-looking package of candy cigarettes was also available. I chose one Bit-O-Honey because I loved the flavor and crunch of peanuts and a Smarties because it had twelve little disks of different sour fruit flavors in one package.

I gave Mrs. Allgeyer the five-dollar bill, and she returned my change. I pocketed the money for safekeeping. I opened the Bit-O-Honey and popped a large piece in my mouth.

Then, carefully lifting the brown paper sack, I cradled it in my arms. I backed into the front door to open it and walked outside into the sunshine. The day seemed a little brighter on that special occasion.

I slowly walked home. My arms grew tired from the weight of the groceries, but I wanted to make the trip last as long as possible. I wanted to make my candy last, too, but I could not resist biting the Bit-O-Honey chunk and having it stick to my teeth like taffy. The wonderful flavor made me forget my caution when again passing the downtrodden house on the corner.

I retraced my steps home, walking as leisurely as possible. Who knew when I might again be allowed to make the journey?

I made the first piece of candy last the entire trip home. I saved the Smarties for later in the day when I could carefully place one piece at a time on my tongue where it would melt in a burst of flavor, before I added a second enjoyable disk.

My wanderlust had been satisfied for that day. I sensed future trips to Allgeyer's could never seem quite as grand as the first trip alone. I would have to find new areas to explore for even greater thrills. I had just begun to discover how large the world was and how much I enjoyed investigating new places.

FAMILY SEPARATION

In many families, life's circumstances sometimes lead to a temporary separation of the family group. This may occur when one adult must go to another town to care for an elderly relative or when a spouse takes a temporary job away from home for an extended period. Kay and I were temporarily separated from our parents in late July and early August 1961.

In the 1960s, the state of Iowa had a regulation that required public school teachers to earn graduate credit hours every few years to maintain their teaching certificates. Mom had delayed obtaining her hours until 1961 because Kay and I had been so young. By the summer of 1961, she had to obtain six hours in order to be able to teach in Winterset that fall.

Mom studied the available graduate school options that she could afford in the nearby area. She also had to enroll in a college or university that offered the curriculum she needed. She settled on Drake University, a private institution in Des Moines about forty-five miles from home and the closest school available.

Her courses required her to be in class for five days a week for two weeks, and she needed the weekends to study. She planned to commute daily to Des Moines with a few other teachers who were also taking courses there. The tuition cost was substantial, but she could earn all of the hours she needed by August.

Mom's quandary was what to do with Kay and me,

ages four and eight. Dad traveled in his job for five to six days a week. The cost of hiring a babysitter for ten to twelve hours a day for so many days a week, as well as pay college tuition, was more than our parents' budget could handle.

My grandparents were not physically able to keep up with two energetic youngsters. My father's only brother lived in Utah, so our staying with him was not an option.

Mom turned to her youngest brother Owen for help. He was five years older than she and owned a farm outside Guilford, Missouri. When she explained the situation to him, he and my Aunt Rose agreed to become temporary parents. They had no children of their own, although my aunt had a grown daughter from a previous marriage.

The morning we were to leave Winterset for two weeks, Mother helped Kay and me pack our needed possessions. Kay took along her favorite stuffed animals, including her teddy bear. I packed some books and my clothes, never being one to play with dolls or stuffed toys. We loaded our bags into the family car and drove about sixty miles south to Mount Ayr, Iowa.

We met Uncle Owen and Aunt Rose at the city park in Mount Ayr, which was about halfway between Winterset and my uncle's farm in Missouri. As we said our good-byes, I could see the sadness in Mom's eyes. I knew she felt she was abandoning her children, even though the separation could not be avoided.

We girls and our possessions were loaded into my uncle and aunt's car. As Mom drove north and we turned south, my sister was crying as she looked out the rear window, already homesick for our mother.

We had been to Uncle Owen's farm many times before, but we had never stayed there for any extended time. We loved our uncle and aunt and did not mind staying with them. That trip, however, was the first time we had been separated from our mother for more than a day or so.

At night, Kay and I slept upstairs in the spare bedroom. The room did not have an air conditioner, so the windows were left open all night and a fan stirred the air. We fell asleep to the occasional barking of my uncle's dog as he stood guard on the farm and its surrounding fields.

In the mornings, as the sun first peeked over the eastern ridge, the pheasants began to call to their mates. Mourning doves and other birds started singing. We could hear cattle mooing, demanding their morning's grain ration. Hogs flipped open the tin feeder lids, which clanked as they dropped shut.

Each day, Kay and I woke with the sunrise. We quickly dressed, then proceeded downstairs and out into the chilly morning air. We watched Uncle Owen and Aunt Rose milk six cows, pour the milk through a filter and into milk cans, and store the cans in a below-ground refrigerated case in the barnyard. Periodically, a driver from the milk company arrived to collect the cans. The milk was pasteurized, packaged, and sent to grocery stores.

After milking, Uncle Owen fed the livestock and checked the watering troughs. Aunt Rose returned to the house, where she prepared a full country breakfast for all of us. Breakfast was sausage, bacon, or sausage gravy; eggs; and biscuits or toast and jam.

For two weeks, Uncle Owen and Aunt Rose tried

to keep us busy. They had a garden, so we ate home-grown vegetables. We even had sweet corn on the cob, dripping with melted butter.

Uncle Owen owned a quarter horse named Duchess. Sometimes, Uncle Owen mounted Duchess and placed me in front of him. Then we rode at a walk down the dirt lane that ran along the south side of his property, and he talked to me about the farm and life.

I was allowed to ride alone as long as Duchess was inside the corral beside the barn. Uncle Owen usually saddled Duchess and, while he and Aunt Rose milked, I rode her. I loved horses, and Duchess was quite tame. She knew when a child was on her back, so she never bucked. Her coloring was a rich brown, and I loved the smell of the leather saddle and reins.

One morning, I was riding Duchess when she grew curious about what was happening inside the barn. She proceeded to walk up the short steep ramp the cows used when they entered the barn to be milked. Duchess placed her head over the closed half of the Dutch door and quietly surveyed the barn's interior. There she stood, resisting my efforts to pull on the reins and make her back down the ramp. Finally, Uncle Owen had to come and lead her back to the corral.

My emotions stayed under control most of the time. I had previously visited my grandparents in Macksburg on weekends and my uncles in Missouri for a day or two.

Kay, being four years younger, experienced true homesickness. She had several crying spells, and it was especially difficult at bedtime not to have Mom present. Aunt Rose read us nighttime stories, but she could not replace our mother.

We all met my parents on Sunday after the first week of separation. We had a picnic, again in the park in Mount Ayr. Seeing Mom, yet knowing we were to be separated again, was almost unbearable. During the week, we had become accustomed to her not being present. Seeing her again made us realize how much we missed her. The difficulty of parting that afternoon was almost worse than it had been the first time we separated the week before.

Mom missed us even more than we missed her. In later years, she admitted that she did not think she could survive the two weeks without us.

Aunt Rose distracted us for two days the following week when she announced she was going to sew us matching shorts and tops. She had some leftover white fabric with a red pattern on it. With the material, she made each of us our new clothes.

Those outfits were the first matching clothes Kay and I had ever worn. Kay often received my hand-me-downs, for I grew so tall so quickly that I seldom could wear the same clothes more than a few months before I outgrew them. In our matching outfits, I almost felt like we were twins, even though we had different personalities.

The high point of our two-week stay occurred when Uncle Owen and Aunt Rose announced, "We're going to take you to the Sidney, Iowa, rodeo." That event was officially sanctioned by the Professional Rodeo Cowboys Association, so the top rodeo cowboys and prime bucking horses and Brahma bulls appeared there. The small town in southwest Iowa drew thousands of people for the event, which lasted several days.

Kay and I dressed in our new matching outfits. We

were all up early so Uncle Owen and Aunt Rose could milk the cows, feed the livestock, and then clean up before we left for the rodeo.

We all climbed into the car and headed northwest from Missouri into Iowa. Along the way, my uncle announced, "You girls can't go to the rodeo without some proper clothes."

He stopped at a clothing store in a small Iowa town. He bought two small, red, straw cowboy hats, one for each of us. The hats even had drawstrings to tighten under our chins so the hats would not blow off in the prairie breezes.

I had always wanted some cowboy boots and a cowboy hat. Now I had the hat and I felt like a real Western cowgirl. I was riding high with pride and ready for a rodeo. We had a wonderful time watching all the bronc and bull riders, steer wrestlers, and clowns.

Two days later, our long separation from our parents ended. My mother completed her college courses and arrived to collect us. We were totally suntanned from spending two weeks on the farm and full of tales about what we had done.

As we hugged and talked, all the bravado displayed by Mom and us girls could not mask how we had all felt, especially my mother. The family was now reunited, and we happily made the trip north toward Winterset and home.

THE CHARTREUSE MONARCH

The day I first saw the chartreuse Monarch bicycle I discovered a sense of freedom that changed my life forever.

One summer's afternoon in 1961 when I was eight years old, Mom called me in from play. She then proceeded to help four-year-old Kay and me clean up.

Washing our faces long before bedtime could only mean we were going somewhere. I did not care where; I just loved adventure.

While my father traveled on the road with his job, Mom had no means of transportation. Our family owned one car, and Dad had possession of it during the workweek. Thus, anywhere Mom, Kay, and I went in town, we walked.

After we passed our mother's inspection, off we went for a trip. We walked one block west, crossed Main Street (Highway 169), and continued west. Finally, we arrived at a stucco-covered house with a large front porch. There it stood—-a chartreuse Monarch girl's bicycle. Mom finalized the details of purchasing the used bike from its current owner. Then she told me the wonderful news that the bicycle was mine.

The lady of the house carefully steered the bicycle off her front porch. The Monarch had thirty-six-inch balloon tires. The bike stood almost as tall as I was, and I was tall for my age.

I gingerly reached over the frame to grasp the cream-colored, rubber, handlebar grips. The bicycle had weight to it. The bicycle represented speed for flying down a road with my hair blowing in the wind. The bicycle was meant for a daredevil who liked to live on the edge. That bicycle was made for me!

Mom watched my facial expression, knowing me well enough to recognize a look of mischief. "I wonder if I made the right choice" was written on her face.

I carefully looked over my Monarch. She had a built-in front light with a three-sided cover. The clear plastic cover on the front lighted the way. A green cover on the right and a red cover on the left allowed the bicycle light to be seen from the sides.

On the frame below the handlebars was the name "Monarch" painted in black letters with gold foil on top. Nearby was the horn button. Behind the cream-colored seat, over the rear wheel guard, was a flat metal covering designed to allow a second person to sit behind the person pedaling. The Monarch was beautiful!

Our family group began our homeward trek. I soon grew restless. I wanted to ride my Monarch. Earlier that summer, I had learned to ride Ray's small child's bike. I just could not wait any longer to try my Monarch.

I halted on the sidewalk and swung my right leg over the bike frame. Slowly resting my right foot on the pedal, I raised myself onto the seat and pushed off with my left foot.

The Monarch frame was so high that my feet barely reached the pedals. I slid off the seat but continued pumping the pedals, trying to get the feel of the weighty machine. The bicycle was well balanced, especially once momentum started propelling me forward.

Heeding Mom's warnings, I proceeded slowly down the sidewalk. The potential for freedom and adventure became evident as I felt the first self-generated breeze caress my face. The bike had definite possibilities. My mind could foresee escaping the bounds of my neighborhood block to explore the rest of my hometown.

I felt the power that wheels could bring. My strong arms guided the wonderful machine down the sidewalk and into the future.

I never noticed that the slope of the sidewalk directed my bike's front wheel toward the left edge. I felt a thump when the front wheel rolled over the sidewalk's edge and into the groove between the concrete and the grass. There my Monarch stayed, even as I tried to guide the wheel back onto the concrete.

I felt like I was in a slow-motion movie as my Monarch and I began falling sideways to the left. My momentum stopped as the bike hit the grass and my head hit a metal water valve protruding from the ground. At first, I didn't feel any pain as I disengaged my legs from the bike, eager to see if it was damaged.

Mom came running up, dragging young Kay behind her. She ignored the bike and grabbed me.

Only then did I notice that the vision in my left eye was becoming blocked. I had the beginnings of a record-setting swollen black eye.

I had hit the water valve directly on the edge of my left eyebrow. The skin between my eyebrow and my eyelash was already beginning to swell, hanging down to cover my eye.

Mom, feeling helpless blocks away from home, surveyed the situation. She had a four-year-old whose legs were tired and who did not want to walk any more. She had an eight-year-old with a black eye. Finally, she had a heavy bicycle to push home.

I assured my mother I was fine and tried to set the bike upright. She helped me, then took Kay's hand. We were determined to make it back home without further mishaps.

From the first day of owning my chartreuse Monarch, my natural wanderlust grew in intensity. I had found the freedom of wheeled mobility. That day also taught me, however, that mobility meant vulnerability. I remembered that lesson only for as long as it took for my eye area to change in color from black, to purple, and then to chartreuse. At least my eye and my bicycle color matched.

The feeling of wind blowing through my hair lasted far longer. I have always loved the sensation of speed and the adventure of travel and have never looked back.

MRS. WILSON

When I was a young girl growing up in the 1950s and 1960s, Mrs. Wilson was already a retired senior citizen. Mrs. Wilson did what she and other seniors of the day were supposed to do, she sat.

She lived in a one-story stucco house, two houses south of my home. The house sat in the middle of the block, facing west onto North Second Street. Across the entire front of the house was an open porch. There Mrs. Wilson sat in her rocker.

Most of the retired folks I knew had rocking chairs. Those were the old-fashioned wooden kind with long runners. When the chair rocked, it took time to roll all the way back on the runners and then all the way forward. The back was tall so that people could rest their head against the slats. Most seniors added cushions to soften the seating for their old bones. Many people pinned hand-embroidered doilies at the top to protect the wood from hair oil.

Mrs. Wilson first emerged onto the porch as soon as the weather warmed in the spring. She rocked as the fresh grass grew and tulips appeared.

In summer's heat, Mrs. Wilson retreated into the house to sit in front of the fan. When cooler evening breezes appeared, however, so did Mrs. Wilson. She said hello to others as they took their evening strolls.

In the fall, Mrs. Wilson watched the hard maple leaves turn colors of flaming red and bright orange. She rocked while neighbors raked leaves and their children flung themselves into the piles. She watched children on their Halloween rounds to all the neighborhood houses. Only when winter's cold forced her inside did she abandon her post.

The house had a small, detached wooden garage. The garage was painted white with a shingled roof, like all the others in the neighborhood. The two doors on the front swung outward. At night, the doors were only latched, never locked. Mrs. Wilson, however, did not have to worry about having her car stolen, since she didn't own one. She rode with "one of the girls" who did have a car.

As with most retired folks, Mrs. Wilson allowed herself one major activity per day. On Mondays, she did laundry. Tuesday mornings meant cards with the girls, usually at Mabel's house. On Wednesday mornings, the ladies' church group met. Thursdays and Fridays were for errands and groceries. Saturdays always found her home, hoping "the kids" would visit and bring the grandchildren. Sundays were for church. Life was orderly.

People in a small town often know everyone else's business. Most people have one best friend to whom they tell all of their daily plans. So did Mrs. Wilson.

Answering machines had not yet been invented and were not needed. If her grown children phoned when she was out, they just called back an hour later. If it were an emergency, they called her best friend Mabel or the church. Someone always knew where she was.

Several retired folks lived on my block. They all cleaned their houses weekly. Their yards (they were never called "lawns") were always immaculate. Most had small gardens, for there was nothing better than fresh baby peas from a garden. They all sat and waited for their grandchildren to visit.

That was many years ago. Two decades later, my parents had an answering machine. They needed one. They still worked part-time because they wanted to keep busy. Each week brought one or two association meetings. Then there were breakfasts with former co-workers, lunches with friends, and birthday parties to celebrate life. The local bank organized one-day bus trips for seniors. Larger tour organizations flooded the postal system with cruise flyers. Everyone under eighty-five and often beyond still drove a car. Satellite television brought the world into their living room. Seniors traveled across the United States in recreational vehicles of various sizes for long periods of time.

We kids never knew where our parents were. We had to leave messages on their answering machine. Otherwise, we called their network of friends, hoping that they were home and knew where our parents had strayed.

Nothing is orderly anymore, and empty rockers sit abandoned on front porches.

SEASONS

I always revered two seasonal events in which the courthouse played a key role. Fall, my favorite season, took center stage around the courthouse. Some of the prettiest hard maple trees in Winterset formed the perimeter of the courthouse grounds. They stood like military sentries, wearing their colorful dress uniforms.

Winterset had some of the most beautiful autumns in the state of Iowa. The hard maple trees all around town produced leaves even larger than my father's hands. When the first frosts of October struck, the tree foliage began the transformation from deep green to hues of banana yellow, bright orange, and blood red.

The leaves became more than mere objects to shade the parked cars of shoppers. The leaves were now vital beings in their own right. Their chromatic contrast against the white limestone of the courthouse created a scene that always made me gasp with delight and awe.

At midnight in the fall, the streets around the town square were silent. The only objects on the otherwise deserted thoroughfares were a few sleeping cars, recuperating after a long day of carrying folks around town. The parking meters stood at attention like rows of silver sentries on duty, protecting the storefronts from the dangers of the night.

Like a lonely prairie coyote hunting in the moonlight, a stray dog occasionally crossed the vastness of the empty streets. The streets seemed to shrink in the daytime from a flood of automobiles and expand at night from loneliness.

The hard maples stood quietly on the town square. The soft melody of their rustling whispered on the night wind. Their song went unnoticed in the daytime bustle of traffic.

Night was the only time when the peace of the town square was protected from the distracting noises created by humans. The square seemed to pause a moment to revel in the wonderful gift of quietness.

* * *

The second event always occurred over a month later. After Thanksgiving, the city fathers installed four strings of holiday lights from the top of the courthouse spire diagonally to a pole at each corner of the square. The lights were large holiday bulbs that filled the town square with color. The best part to me, however, was returning to Winterset at night and watching the lights from miles away.

The holiday lights at the courthouse could be seen for nearly fifteen miles in most directions. Because Winterset sits on a flat area with just a little rise, the lights at night served as a homing beacon for local folks who might have been out of town visiting relatives all day.

As I grew and took jobs out of state, I always looked forward to the last portion on my long drive home for Christmas. The many road miles produced a weariness, suddenly relieved when I topped a ridge and saw the beckoning colored courthouse lights. My car wanted to speed faster to reach town and the enjoyment of the holiday season with relatives.

Those electric colors brought comfort, and I knew I would soon arrive home, tucked safely in my own bed.

The yearly lights were a symbol that life was safe, never ending, and never changing in its important aspects of friends and family. The colors were a visual security blanket for traveling souls who were homebodies at heart.

PLAYING CROKINOLE

My grandfather was a farmer who believed in work, but he allowed himself time for one favorite activity, playing crokinole. When I was a child, crokinole was the only game we ever played together.

Grandpa Lyle was a quiet man. In my entire life, I never heard him raise his voice. He farmed about 160 acres in Madison County, once served on the Macksburg School Board, and occasionally sold insurance. Like most Iowa farmers, he engaged in few frivolous activities. He did, however, attend important events like the Madison County Fair and often the Iowa State Fair.

At home, he read or watched some television. By the time I was born, glaucoma was destroying his eyesight in one eye. I could never tell which eye because he never mentioned the problem, and it never seemed to interfere with his daily activities.

When I visited on weekends or in the summer, one leisure activity Grandpa allowed himself was playing crokinole. This was an old-fashioned board game, from which the modern game of carrom was probably developed. Grandpa's crokinole game board, about two and a half feet wide, was made of wood with octagonal sides. Around the edge ran a rim about an inch high. Just inside the rim was a shallow trough about a quarter of an inch deep below the main board surface.

Like a dart board, the crokinole board had four concentric rings with three tiny grooves in the wood forming the divisions between the rings. The rings were separated into four equal sections with a thin groove extending from the board's center to the outer ring edge. Each of the three inner rings was about three inches in diameter, with the outer fourth ring about one inch wide.

In the center of the board, a circular depression slightly wider than the game pieces had been drilled and lined with felt on the bottom. Surrounding the inner circle but set about an inch into the inner ring were six small metal posts with rubber padding around them. When a game piece hit a post, it bounced off.

The game pieces were wooden disks called buttons about an inch in diameter. Twelve disks were painted black and twelve left the natural wood color. Each player had a set of twelve disks, or four people could play in two teams with each person having six pieces. During play, the participants used their fingers to flick the buttons onto the game board, much like marble players shoot marbles.

Grandpa and I played when I came to visit. We set up the crokinole board on my Grandma's prized dining room table, first ensuring we placed a tablecloth under the board to protect the table's surface from scratches. We found the disks and decided who would have the brown or the black ones. Then we agreed on who would start. Grandpa enjoyed having me start because then he could shoot my pieces off the board.

The object of crokinole was to have the highest score at the end of the game. That usually meant having the most pieces left on the board after the players had shot all their disks.

At the end of the game, any piece remaining in the first outer ring was worth five points, the next ring ten, and the inner ring was fifteen. The player who could shoot a disk to fall exactly into the center depression earned twenty-five points.

I began to play crokinole by placing one button on the outer rim. Bracing the thumbnail of my middle finger against the inside end of my thumb, I flicked my middle finger out against the disk, sending it sliding onto the game board. I aimed for the middle spot, where I hoped the piece would drop into the hole, though it rarely did. The game took practice to learn the amount of force needed to stop the button precisely where desired.

Even if I didn't hit the center depression, I tried to make the piece stop against one of the metal posts. The button would have some protection from the disks shot by Grandpa in an effort to hit mine off the board.

After I played, Grandpa moved his button within his allotted outer ring arc until he could aim and shoot his against mine. If his piece hit mine correctly, my disk slid across the board into the outer trough. The goal was to simultaneously hit my button off the board while leaving his in a good scoring position.

Once any portion of a piece touched the outer ring, the button was considered out of the game. We then pushed it into the trough.

As we played, the buttons began to accumulate on the game board. That was a detriment. When I shot my disk to hit Grandpa's, his piece might bounce into one or more of mine, sending all of them out of play into the trough.

I loved to watch Grandpa's hands as he played. He had large hands with long graceful fingers. His palms had been worn and calloused from years of farming activities. His palms felt like smooth firm leather, and he had a farmer's strong handshake. Yet, with all his strength, he could apply just the right amount of pressure to stop his button where he desired.

Even with his failing eyesight, Grandpa was an expert at crokinole. He understood that the game used the physics of banking to bounce one button off another disk. The banking in crokinole was similar to many of the same principles billiards players use to bounce pool balls off one side of the pool table and into another ball or pocket. Often, with one shot, Grandpa hit three of my buttons off the board at the same time.

When I became a teenager, my grandfather was blind in one eye and had poor eyesight in the second one. He could no longer distinguish the natural-brown buttons from the faded black buttons. I would point to each button on the board and say, "This, this, and this are yours, and that and that are mine." Grandpa would promptly shoot his button, scattering all of mine into the trough or completely off the game board. His skill at the game never diminished.

Grandpa did love to win at crokinole. His facial expression changed little, as he was never one to display much emotional excitement. The corners of his mouth, however, curled slightly into a grin and his eyes twinkled with delight when he won.

As competitive by nature as I was, I never minded losing to Grandpa. He was a superb crokinole player, having played all his life. Each time we played, I knew it would be difficult to beat him.

I never had the feeling that Grandpa let me win. He made me try my best but did not seem to mind when, occasionally, I did beat him. Perhaps he let me win once in a while to keep me interested in the game and in playing with him, but I doubt it.

THE SLEDDING HILL

Since 1870, Great-grandpa Morley owned a small farm near Macksburg. After Great-grandpa Morley died in 1926, Grandpa inherited the land and added more acreage. To Kay and me, the most valuable part of his farm was the sledding hill.

The starting point for the sledding hill began just north of the windbreak surrounding his farmhouse and barnyard. In summer, the hillside was covered in pasture grass. In winter, the slope wore a blanket of snow.

Often the harsh winter gusts blew the snow off the sledding hill. Sometimes, a snowstorm dropped too much snow, causing the sled to sink into the snow and not slide down the hill as desired. Only occasionally did weather conditions create a perfect sledding day.

Ideal sledding snow is about six inches deep, with a slightly icy crust on top. This allows for maximum speed with some steering control by the rider. If there is too much ice on top, a rider has no steering traction and goes down a hill too fast.

One winter's day, Dad, Kay, and I stood on the precipice, sleds poised, facing into the northwest wind. Below its gentle top slope, the hill's angle quickly sharpened. The hill sloped at an angle steep enough to send a child's adrenaline flowing. The entire slope ran for about a quarter of a mile.

Grandpa had kept two sleds from my father's childhood. One sled was over five feet long. Dad could lie on top of it, fully stretched out on his stomach. Since

Kay was four years younger than I was, she was small enough to lie on top of my father's back, holding onto his shoulders. She let him do the steering as they slid down the hill piggy-back. I rode the other three-foot-long sled by myself.

When one final moment of indecision passed, I began running across the hilltop. Tossing the sled on the ground, I threw myself on top of the sled and began the downhill run.

To have the ideal sledding snow with an icy crust on top, the day had to be bone-chillingly cold. I was bundled in my full winter's attire of wool coat, hat, mittens, long pants, and boots. A thick scarf wrapped around my neck and covered the lower portion of my face.

As I raced down the slope, however, the scarf inevitably slipped off my face. Blasts of bitterly cold wind froze my skin. The windchill formed ice on my eyelashes, forcing me suddenly to pop open my eyes so I could continue to see where I was going.

By midpoint down the hill, the sled gained momentum, racing far too fast for me to change my mind about the wisdom of taking the ride. Once the sledding run began, the ride did not end until I reached the foot of the hill.

I felt thrilled by the challenge yet afraid of the speed. I was flying on a magic carpet yet clinging to the sled to remain grounded to the earth. Adrenaline pulsed through my veins. The rapidly approaching scenery flashed by in a blur.

The tall pasture grasses, coated with ice, shattered into splinters of tiny frozen knives that stung my face as the sled crashed through the stalks. I had to open my eyes to steer, yet shards of ice forced them closed again. Cold wind and ice crystals numbed my face. I faced the bitter elements in a hurl of speed and adrenaline.

At the bottom, the land flattened out for a short distance. I had to turn the sled quickly to avoid falling over the three-foot high edge onto a small, dry, rocky creek bed. If the snow crust was too icy, I could not turn in time to avoid dropping over the rim. That day, by using all my small girl's strength, I managed to turn the sled's guides in time.

The sled's momentum eventually slowed, then stopped. The bottom of the hill always arrived too soon. I gasped for warm air. The steep ride had driven the winter's cold air deep into my lungs. My face felt completely iced from the windchill.

My heart, however, raced with excitement. I loved speed.

A steep sledding hill can teach children much about life. The steering skills they learn and enjoyment of speed make them eager for the thrill of driving too fast in a car. Parents do not appreciate those talents.

The thrill of a steep slope can also satisfy the daredevil nature of many children but in a somewhat controlled environment. Parents can even join their children, if they are not afraid to speed down the hills with them.

The best sledding hill can teach one of life's most important lessons. From the bottom of a hill, the top appears a long distance away. To enjoy another ride, however, the sledder must climb back to the top.

Even some of life's most thrilling and enjoyable times require great effort. The view from the summit and the thrill of the run down, however, are worth the successful struggle up the hill.

THE FIRE ESCAPE

I could hardly wait to begin third grade in the fall of 1961. My eagerness had nothing to do with becoming older and facing new challenges in class. My desire had everything to do with the privilege accorded to third and fourth grade students at North Ward Elementary School. Those grades were taught to use the second-floor fire escape chute during fire drills.

North Ward was a large, square, dark-red brick building. On the ground floor were two classes each of first and second grade students. Up the wide, highly polished, wooden stairs on the second floor were two classes each of third and fourth graders and the principal's office. Only when students had advanced up the lofty staircase to third grade could they use the fire escape.

The enclosed fire escape chute was attached to the north side of the school and looked like a gigantic aluminum paper towel tube. Starting on the northwest fourth-grade room on the second floor, the chute extended out from the wall about four feet. Then it made a ninety-degree turn, angling down toward the ground. At its lower end, the chute leveled out about three feet to a door that was closed except when school was in session.

At the beginning of the year, Mr. Leonard Mains, the principal, addressed each new third grade class. He explained the proper procedure for using the fire escape and closely supervised students in each class as they practiced descending the chute.

Upon hearing the fire alarm, each class was to file in an orderly manner along a prescribed path to the fourth-grade room in which Mom taught. There, we were to form a single-file line along the east and north walls of the classroom. The entrance to the fire escape chute was covered by a door in Mom's classroom. She would open the door and signal the student at the head of the line to be ready to enter and slide down the chute. Each classroom's teacher descended the chute first to catch her students as they exited the chute. One teacher remained in the room ensure all students were out of the second floor, then slid down herself.

When it was my turn, I grasped the metal bar across the top of the chute's opening. The dark chute looked like a huge, toothless snake's mouth.

I then swung my legs into the chute's blackened interior and released the bar. The interior of the chute was highly polished aluminum, just like an ordinary school playground slide. Once I released my hands, I was sliding down the chute in total darkness. From the top of the fire escape, I could not see the lower exit's opening.

The fire escape chute required a literal leap of faith into the darkness by each student. The first time down the chute, each child had to make several assumptions. First, the student had to believe there was, indeed, an opening below since no light was visible from the top. Second, the child had to assume that the lower door had been opened that day and the students sliding down were not piled together in one mangled heap at the darkened bottom. Third, the student had to have faith that a teacher really would slow his or her descent at the bottom exit for, while sliding down, one quickly built up speed.

Mr. Mains had instructed us to spread our feet apart as we descended the chute. We were gently to brace our feet against the sides of the fire escape to slow our rate of descent. If we did so properly, we slid down safely and did not slam into the back of the student who had descended before us.

I only required one practice slide down the fire escape to become hooked on its speed and adventure. I liked the thrill of grasping the bar, flinging my body into the darkness, and shooting out the bottom two stories below. I quickly concluded that we would never have enough fire drills to satisfy me.

Being a teacher's child and raised to obey the rules, I did as Mr. Mains instructed, at least to some extent. During the initial descent, however, I kept my legs together to gain maximum speed down the chute. I did not brace my feet until I neared the bottom. I managed to slow myself just in time to avoid sliding into the student in front of me.

I was never brave enough to flaunt completely the rules of descent as some did. During a practice session, one boy never braced his legs. He always slid sharply into the student in front of him at the lower opening, sending both of them flying into the air before smacking onto the ground on their posteriors.

The boy appeared to be dutifully sorry when Mr. Mains explained to him that he had to repeat the practice run. One day, to his great enjoyment, the boy managed to take three practice rides down before his rear end began to ache from the rough landings.

In each new third grade class, one or two students would be truly afraid of the fire escape. Then, Mr. Mains or a teacher sat the student in front of him or her and both practiced sliding down together. Usually, those joint slides helped the student overcome any fears.

We never knew when the practice fire drills might occur. Only Mr. Mains was allowed to pull the fire alarm. We were, however, guaranteed at least one drill during National Fire Prevention Week in early October each year. Then the local fire department also sent a real firefighter (always a man since no women were hired) to the school to talk about fire prevention and safety. A fire truck was parked outside the building.

As students, we understood the importance and seriousness of fire drills. Luckily, our school never had a real fire. I continued to enjoy the practice drills for two years. My greatest disappointment about growing up and going to fifth grade in another school building was giving up the thrill of descending our fire escape chute.

THE WINDSHIELD

Tommy Thompson was the second generation of his family to supply coal and fuel oil to Winterset citizens. To a great extent, unless their homes had electric furnaces, each winter the welfare of many Winterset residents rested on his prompt delivery service. Otherwise, older people especially might not survive the bitterly cold nights.

When I was almost nine in late fall of 1961, I once accompanied my father into Tommy's store on the town square. The store was located in a red brick building with a very high ceiling and two large plate glass windows facing Court Street. Inside were fuel oil heaters and other types of stoves Tommy sold at retail. He also owned a dump truck to deliver coal and a small tanker for dispensing fuel oil.

On that day, Tommy began to expound on his childhood. Around 1908, when Tommy was around eight years old, his father bought one of the first Model T automobiles ever to drive on Winterset streets. Most people at that time still rode in horse-drawn buggies and buckboards.

Tommy's father drove the car for a while. Then one day he proudly announced that he was going to Des Moines the next morning to buy a windshield.

In the early 1900s, parents never bothered to explain much to their offspring. Tommy's imagination led him to speculate on what a windshield could possibly be. He knew of no one in Winterset who owned a car with a windshield, and he had never heard the word.

Only three reasons existed for anyone to make the nearly forty-mile trek to Des Moines, the Iowa capital. The most common reason was a severe illness or injury that the Winterset doctors could not treat and required a large hospital staff's care. Usually, such a trip indicated to the patient that he might be near death, possibly leading to the patient's demise from sheer fright.

The second reason was to attend the annual Iowa State Fair in August. The buggy trip to the east side of Des Moines took all day. The few farm families who attended often camped in tents on the fairgrounds and stayed a day or two. Then they made the long ride back home.

Third, folks traveled to Des Moines if they had business with the state legislature. Of course, no one could remember anyone in Winterset ever needing the meddling of politicians enough to request their assistance.

Thus, Tommy concluded, a windshield must be a fourth purpose serious enough to necessitate such a trip. For the remainder of that day, all night, and all the next day, Tommy speculated on what a windshield could be.

Obviously, a windshield was a costly item, which required his father's taking a day off from work to obtain it personally. Also, the object had to be able to fit into the Model T, since his father had driven off in his automobile that morning. The Model T had only two front seats, a two-person back seat, and a small trunk, so a windshield had to fit into one of those spaces.

Despite his best attempts, Tommy never arrived at a logical conclusion. As the hours dragged by slowly, Tommy's curiosity grew. He could think of nothing else, did not even have an interest in eating, and never bothered to play that day.

Evening neared before Tommy heard his father's Model T pulling up to the house. Tommy rushed outside to see the marvelous invention called a windshield.

His father stepped down proudly from his automobile. With a flourish of his arm, he pointed to his expensive new windshield.

Tommy skidded to a stop in shock. A windshield was just a piece of glass resting in a metal frame in front of the dashboard.

His hopes, speculations, and wonder had come to that disappointing conclusion. What was so special about a piece of glass?

I listened to the man in his sixties recount his tale. I began to realize I wasn't the only child in the world who was often confused because adults did not explain life's mysteries. Adults who seemed to have all the answers had to learn along life's road what they knew as grownups.

I left the store a little less in awe of adults. I realized that even trying to reason out a situation could leave people with the wrong conclusions. Often, they just had to see a curiosity to define its reality, and sometimes reality was just a piece of glass.

THE LAST SANTA

Kay and I grew up, like most American children, believing in Santa Claus. Each year we looked forward to December because it meant Christmas was coming.

Even as a child, religion and I never merged, so the holiday season to me represented Santa more than a child in a manger. It was not about material possessions as such, but more because my birthday was only six days before Christmas. I, thus, waited an entire year, 359 days, to receive any presents at all. Most kids I knew had at least one other day in a different month when they got gifts to celebrate their birthday. My gifts arrived within a week of each other, or not at all.

Winterset was a small town, so we usually did not see Santa Claus uptown or at a store. Even Des Moines, where we occasionally shopped, did not have many "Santa's helpers" for children to visit. We, therefore, knew that the real Santa only came Christmas Eve to our living room to add his gifts under our tree.

Our family's Christmas tree sometimes looked more like a Charlie Brown tree than the tall, dense, long-needled fir we saw depicted in magazines. At least we had one, under which Mom spread a blanket to catch the falling needles and to hold the family presents. Kay and I understood that our parents gave us some of the Christmas gifts, because the tags said "Mom and Dad." But Santa brought the good stuff, the seriously special presents for which we asked each year.

Money was always tight, so we sisters knew not to ask for too many presents. We never made out Christmas lists, for past experience indicated we only got a few items, so we had better choose carefully what we requested.

Christmas presents came in two categories: practical and desired. Mostly our parents' gifts to us were the practical ones. Those might be clothes, a board or card game to encourage memory and following directions, and maybe something homemade. Santa's presents might be one or two of the things we desired with all our young hearts. Never too expensive, bordering on practical at times, but treasured because Santa brought them.

Each Christmas Eve, Kay and I had to be asleep before midnight or Santa would not stop at our house. Our usual bedtime was around eight o'clock, but the thrill of Santa and presents to open in the morning often made it hard for us to descend into dreamland.

The week I turned nine, I was in bed at the appointed time and had drifted into sleep. Something, some noise, woke me. I lay silently in my bed, barely breathing. Perhaps I had slept until midnight and Santa was in the living room leaving our presents.

Quietly, I crept out of bed. My parents had left the bedroom door slightly open. I tiptoed across the wooden floor, praying no board would creak, and laid my eye against the door crack. In the living room, I saw—not Santa—but my parents placing the last few wrapped packages under the tree. The ones from Santa always laid on top on Christmas morning when Kay and I rushed to the living room. Those presents now being placed had to be ones from "Santa."

Heartbroken, I crept back to bed. No Santa. Santa Claus did not exist. Everyone had lied to me all my nine years, because there was no Santa Claus, only my parents giving us gifts with "Santa" on the tag. How many other treasured characters, like the Easter Bunny and the Tooth Fairy, were fakes, too?

A woman I knew in college once described her disillusionment about Santa Claus. She was the oldest of her siblings and had asked her mother if Santa was real. Her mother had always replied, "Santa is the spirit of giving." When the woman finally had her moment of revelation, she, too, felt extremely disappointed. Then she remembered her mother's words that Santa was the spirit of giving to others. Somehow, the truth, while shattering her childhood dreams, proved easier to accept when considering what Santa truly represented.

As the years have passed, the myth of Santa Claus has continued to be instilled in children. I still see it as a good story, something to be encouraged for as long as the fantasy can be continued. Children will find out the truth eventually.

In the meantime, they are encouraged to behave during the stressful holidays because Santa is watching. They are asked to share their abundance, however much that may be, with others who have less. They are taught to be kind to others, even if it is only for one month a year. The spirit of giving is worth telling our children a wonderful tale of hope and kindness, even if a little white lie is involved.

LOST INNOCENCE

In 1962, winter had again covered Iowa in ankle-deep snow. I was nine years old and in third grade when the icy cold of early March arrived.

My mother taught fourth grade in the mornings at North Ward Elementary School, where I attended. North Ward was located in the east-central part of Winterset. Then she ate lunch and drove southwest of downtown, where South Ward Elementary School and Winterset Junior High School were combined in one large building, collectively known as South Ward. There, Mom taught physical education to junior high girls in the afternoon. She parked her car on the street and walked up steep steps and a long sidewalk to enter the junior high portion of the building.

On March 1, my third-grade class had just returned from lunch. As we noisily settled into our seats for our afternoon lessons, Mr. Leonard Mains, our principal, entered the room.

To my complete embarrassment, Mr. Mains headed for my desk in sight of my classmates. No student had a personal visit from the principal, especially in his or her own homeroom, unless something quite serious had occurred.

Mr. Mains leaned down and told me to report to his office after school. I immediately turned white and froze in my seat.

I was a teacher's child. I was required to behave perfectly at school, or I would regret it when I returned home. My teachers knew my parents believed in proper behavior, so I never pulled any pranks in class. Of course, I never tried anything, either, because I knew my mother would immediately hear what I had done. She taught in the same building.

During that interminable afternoon, I worried. I could not concentrate on my lessons. All I could do was try to imagine what I had done to be called to the principal's office. At morning and lunch recesses, nothing special had occurred. I had not acted up in class that morning. For what action could I possibly be in trouble?

By three o'clock, my nerves were in one big knot. My stomach felt tight and queasy. No matter how much I thought, I had not found a reason why the principal wanted to see me.

My homeroom was on the southeast corner of North Ward's second floor. The principal's office was located centrally at the opposite side of the building. Between the two rooms stretched a long corridor with a polished wood floor. The sun reflected off the shiny wood in the late afternoon.

My walk down the corridor was the longest of my life. I waited until my classmates rushed off after school, so they would not see my humiliation at having to go to the principal's office.

I slowly dragged my feet along the corridor. I tried to take small steps, but the principal's office kept coming nearer and nearer. Finally, I knocked on his door.

Mr. Mains called me in and offered me a seat. I slid into the polished wooden chair, resting my hands in my lap. My eyes stared up at him. That was it, my final moments before sentencing.

"Your mother slipped on the ice at South Ward and broke her hip," were Mr. Mains' first words to me.

"She's in the Winterset hospital, but she's going to be fine."

My first reaction was one of glee. All I could think about was I was not in trouble with the principal! I sat in the chair, almost breaking into the biggest smile of my life.

Then the true reality of the situation settled into my consciousness. My mother was badly hurt. Tears threatened to fall from my eyes.

The woman who babysat Kay and me after school lived several blocks from the school. She happened to live across the street from Mr. Mains, so he gave me a ride that afternoon. That was the first time I had ever ridden in a principal's car.

Kay attended half-day, morning kindergarten classes, so she was already at the babysitter's house. We waited anxiously for our father's return.

As had happened the day I was born, Dad was working out of town. The Iowa Highway Patrol had been notified to locate him and tell him about his wife's injury. They did so, and he rushed to the hospital late in the day.

Early that evening, Dad arrived to collect his two tired, scared daughters and take us home. My father usually arrived home in the evenings after we girls were in bed. That night, I had to take charge of the bedtime routine, since I was more familiar with the schedule.

The hospital had a strict policy about children under age twelve not being allowed to visit patients, so we could not see Mom for several days. Forced to sit for hours in the hospital waiting room, we tried to concentrate on reading books. I could not, so I studied the pale green of the hospital walls and darker green of the plastic covers on the chairs. Green tiles with small colored specks covered the floors. The waiting room did not have a television. The hospital's antiseptic smells did nothing to cheer our long evenings.

Kay and I were never truly sure that Mom was alive. Always the hidden fear that the grownups in our world were not telling us the truth needled our thoughts. We needed to see our mother for ourselves to calm our fears.

Finally, when Mom had been in the hospital for several days and would be there even longer, some of the nurses relented. In the evenings, they allowed Kay and me quietly to hurry down the darkened hospital corridor to Mom's room. We could talk to her and wonder when our world would return to normal.

The following days and weeks brought confusion and an upset daily routine. Kay and I continued in school, trying to concentrate as best as we could. Family friends brought casseroles and other food to the house. One couple invited Dad, Kay, and me to their home for a meal.

All the family roles became altered. Previously, Mom had prepared breakfast, done the housework, shopped for groceries, and reared her daughters. Dad's work kept him on the road most of the time, so he was present mainly on the weekends.

Mothering did not come naturally to my father. While friends promptly arrived with food for evening meals, we were at the mercy of Dad's cooking skills when it came to breakfast.

Normally, Kay and I had cereal and toast for breakfast, or maybe scrambled eggs. Dad's idea of the perfect breakfast for the next several weeks was oatmeal with raisins—every morning. Day in and day out. And I had never cared much for oatmeal. Soon, I began to dread the idea of rising in the morning, because I had to face that light brown, glutenous stuff at the bottom of my bowl.

I now had to prepare my own school lunches. Our food supplies were limited in variety, including mostly peanut butter, Velveeta cheese, bread, and some packaged cookies. One of my experiments with lunch variety became a peanut butter, sliced bananas, and mayonnaise sandwich. I learned I would not make that combination again—ever.

Caring for our hair became a major issue for me. Kay, age five, had naturally straight hair, so it was easy for me to wash her hair and comb it out. My hair was naturally curly and wavy. Mom had always set my curls with bobby pins, wrapping each hair strand deftly in a spiral before pinning it in place to dry. Suddenly, at age nine, I was faced with either learning to set my own hair or facing my classmates with a mass of disorganized fuzz on my head.

My first attempts at curling my hair proved disastrous. No matter how wet I got a strand, it refused to curl several times around my finger so I could press it against my head and lock it in place with a bobby pin. Over and over I tried to do what Mom had done so easily. My young fingers seemed to lack the dexterity to make my hair conform. Tears of frustration flowed quietly.

Although lovingly concerned for Mom's hospital stay and unknown recovery period, I was angry at her for putting me in that position. At age nine, I was too young to care for myself, let alone try to be a mother figure to Kay. I was now doing the dishes, setting the table, getting Kay and me bathed, fixing my own school lunches, and attempting to learn the frustrating task of setting my hair. It was too much to ask! Life wasn't fair!

Finally, I succeeded in getting one strand bound under a pin. I stared into the small mirror sitting on the kitchen counter. Yes, the pin looked like it would hold. I tried another strand and another and another. I couldn't see the back of my head, so I had to remember the feel of my mother's curling and pinning to set the hardest part of my hair. I dried my hair by turning my head back and forth so the small hand dryer that sat on the counter blew onto the dense curls.

I slept on the bobby pins that night, then combed out the curls in the morning before school. The results were presentable, if not perfect. I could face the school day looking nearly normal.

The accident changed our family's dynamics. Dad was forced to continue helping with household chores for weeks to come while my mother recovered at home. I no longer needed Mom's help fixing my hair, a task she later admitted she missed dreadfully, for a part of our special time together had disappeared. Her eldest daughter had been forced to grow up before she should have. Kay had survived as best she could between the feeble attempts at mothering by our father and me.

My childhood innocence about life and death ceased one cold March day. I was a true daredevil at heart, a tomboy willing to risk my own life in childhood games. The adults in my world, however, were supposed to be immortal. My mother's accident proved they were not.

All children lose their innocence at some point in time. I would have preferred my loss to have been much later. I did not have a vote in the matter. None of us do.

MULTIPLICATION AND EASTER EGGS

A schoolteacher never knows what trigger will motivate a student. Sometimes the simplest and least expensive token will fire a student's eagerness to learn.

My third-grade school year from fall 1961 through spring 1962 involved serious efforts at learning to do more complicated multiplication problems. All that year, we students had been learning our tables. By spring, when I was nine years old, we were up to the sevens, eights, and nines.

I adored my homeroom and mathematics teacher, Mrs. Stark, as I had all my teachers thus far. She was a short woman with gray hair, a kind smile, and a frequent laugh. She had great patience, which she needed with our class of bright talkative students.

Mrs. Stark had gradually brought our learning process along, pulling us through the lower numbers of the multiplication tables. At the same time, we were expected to learn long division, too. Many of the students considered both assaults too much to learn simultaneously.

With various visual aids, Mrs. Stark explained the concepts of math. She frequently showed us a chart to teach us that numbers have patterns in multiplication results.

With her multiplication chart, the numbers zero through nine were written down the left side. The same numbers were written from left to right across the top of the chart. The horizontal and vertical line intersections from any two numbers provided the multiplication result. For example, finding six on the left side and moving horizontally to connect with the line coming down from five at the top meant the multiplication answer was 30.

The best part of math class was when Mrs. Stark allowed us to have multiplication races. Two students approached the blackboard, which was actually dark green in color. With chalk in hand, they waited tensely for Mrs. Stark to read off the first number. The instant she announced the second number, the two competitors frantically wrote down the number, drew a horizontal line underneath, and rapidly worked out the multiplication answer. The first student to lay down his or her chalk and have the correct answer was the winner.

Sometimes we held multiplication king-of-the-hill contests. In those, the student with the correct answer could stay at the blackboard. As long as the student continued to answer correctly, he or she stayed in the game. The long-term winner continued to face all challengers, at least until the class period ended.

Being quite competitive by nature, I adored the math races. At multiplication, I had only one serious rival, Bill. He, too, was an excellent student, but often his mind raced faster than his hand. Bill sometimes wrote down the wrong answer, even when he knew the right one. Sometimes his handwriting was so poor that Mrs. Stark could not read the answer, so she declared the legible writer, but second place finisher, to be the winner.

We held similar races for division, but all the students were much slower at those than at multiplication. I preferred multiplication to division, considering division too time and brainpower consuming to be useful.

Even with all of Mrs. Stark's teaching techniques, I was still having trouble learning my sevens, eights, and nines on the multiplication tables. In March 1962, my mother had broken her hip, so our family life was still in some confusion. The entire class also had a serious attack of spring fever as Easter drew near and the weather began to warm.

Thus, we all seemed to slow down in learning multiplication. Mrs. Stark's lesson plan schedule was at risk of being delayed due to general malaise by her students. The time had come for a creative solution from her teacher's bag of tricks.

The answer came in the form of Easter candy. Just after Easter that year, Mrs. Stark arrived at math class with an announcement. Her family had leftover Easter egg candy.

Two pieces would be awarded to each student who learned the sevens, two more for the eights, and two more for the nines. To prove one had learned the math tables, each student had to recite to Mrs. Stark the entire zero through nine multiplication for each of the three numbers.

I was in heaven and willing to learn, for candy was a great motivator for me. The candy was Brach's three-inch long, hard-shelled Easter eggs. Those were the kind with the brightly colored candy covering a white marshmallow inner core. The lime-flavored outer shell was my favorite. Each egg came individually wrapped in cellophane, just waiting for an eager student like me to tear into it.

The sevens proved little challenge. I managed them in a day. The eights were harder, but I soon conquered them. The nines were caught in my mental fog.

Finally, that multiplication chart began to make sense. The pattern began to appear in my brain. Nine times three was twenty-seven. Nine times four was thirty-six. Once I knew one starting combination, the next higher combination involved increasing the left number by one and decreasing the right number by one. Nine times five was forty-five. Once the key appeared, I learned the nines in short order.

Since I was always a candy-holic, I was supremely pleased to gather my prizes. My family had little candy around the house, so I practically drooled when walking by the shelves of candy bars in the grocery store. Yet, in school, Mrs. Stark gave away candy just for learning. I decided I was going to like school.

If all my subsequent teachers had followed Mrs. Stark's simple enticement, I would have been a much better student in physics and chemistry courses. I will always remember how easy learning multiplication tables was when my teacher used a simple form of bribery to motivate me to study harder. Sometimes a bribe can be as small as a candy Easter egg.

ESCAPE TO CAMP

Some children dread being sent to summer camp. I longed for it. In my small town in the mid-1960s, few activities were available for children during the summer. We took swimming lessons and enjoyed books from the library. Beyond that, we were left to our own creativity with neighborhood children to invent excitement.

I had joined Camp Fire Girls a couple of years earlier and had enjoyed the group meetings. We sold Camp Fire candy to raise funds to support the organization nationally and locally. We learned crafts and earned badges that we proudly sewed onto blue vests that we had to purchase. We wore red neck scarves that we learned to tie in a square knot to hang at our chest.

Camp Fire Girls also held weekly summer camp sessions on a large acreage outside Boone, Iowa. Such a chance for something to do in June sounded wonderful, but I doubted my family could afford to send me.

My parents, however, surprised me. They said I could go!

We applied for a first and second choice of camp session. A response letter provided my acceptance dates and listed items to bring. We began collecting the required clothes, toiletries, and bug spray. My excitement soared as the day to arrive at camp neared.

My parents, Kay, and I loaded the car and drove to Boone, nearly sixty miles north. I was truly going away to camp far from home. My first big adventure was beginning.

We drove through the upright gate with the Hantesa camp name on top and up a grassy lane to the main camp buildings. The camp registration area was the usual chaos of arriving campers, their well-wishing relatives, and cars coming and going. I got registered and assigned to a "cabin" with five other girls.

After we deposited my suitcase and bedding on my cot, my parents said goodbye. Only one other time in my life had I ever spent an entire week apart from both parents. I felt thrilled at the adventures to come, yet anxious about the separation.

Our cabin was a wooden platform raised three feet off the ground. Wooden posts held up the roof. The sides were wood from the floor upward for three feet, then open except for screening to deter flying insects. We learned how to make square corners when folding our sheets, and each day, we were required to make our beds.

As the week passed, I enjoyed new activities every day. I had swimming lessons in the large outdoor pool. I gathered leaves and pressed them, placing them in a small portfolio to take home at the end of the week. I even learned archery and found that I had a little natural talent for it. The camp food was great, and we could have all we wanted.

Evenings were spent enjoying sing-along sessions, watching stars, and sitting around campfires. Each cabin had its own counselor, and I adored ours. She played folk songs on her guitar at night as we snuggled into bed. By bedtime, we gladly sank into sleep, being tired from all the day's activities. Someone even played "Taps" on a bugle each evening at lights out time, the lingering emotional notes floating across camp on the still night air.

Cabin areas were grouped by the ages of the camp- ers. The entire camp had a daily contest to determine the cleanest, neatest cabins in each section. While we ate breakfast in the communal mess hall, several ad- ministrators visited all cabins and judged the results.

At the end of breakfast, the first, second, and third place winners for each age group were announced. Outside each cabin was a vertical post four inches in diameter and four feet high. The first-place winners proudly got to paint a blue stripe around their post. The second-place winners painted a yellow and the third-place winners received a red stripe. For the en- tire week, my cabin won blue every day! We were so proud and so careful about how we maintained our living quarters.

I knew the days were passing quickly. Soon the time to return home neared. I felt sorrow at having to leave the camp where I had had so much fun and men- tal stimulation. I was not ready to go home.

My parents arrived at the appointed day and time. We loaded my belongings into the car, and Mom was misty-eyed at seeing me again.

I, too, was misty-eyed but for a very different reason. As the car passed under the entry gate, I looked back at the camp. My eyes had tears of sadness at leaving my first summer's camping session. I wanted more, for I had truly needed the mental stimulation and activities to keep me busy during the summer. When I got home and discovered I had left my leaf portfolio at camp, my loss was compounded.

Children need unstructured time to use their imag- inations and to explore the world without strict rules. Too many parents, however, feel the need to schedule every moment of their children's lives in group activities. A balance must be found between free play time and regulated events. Camp provided that balance.

Children do need mental challenges even in summer to keep their minds growing and active. Camps provide one source of such stimulation. I am glad to see communities offering more summer activities, whether day or week camps. I wish we had had more such activities for our town when I was young.

THE CHINA HUTCH

Every August, the Iowa State Fair reappears for eleven days in Des Moines. It is one of the largest and most well-known state fairs in the United States, first opening in 1854. As the fair is the most exciting annual event for many in Iowa, entire families save their money to attend. They carefully study the program in the newspaper to plan the perfect day for their trip.

For my family, the fair was only fifty miles away, but a world apart in adventure. As a young girl in the mid-1960s, I could not imagine anything I wanted more than to attend the fair.

Exhibitors displayed canning and floral design projects, live beehives, farm equipment, and mechanical innovations. Stock barns held prize-winning horses, cows, hogs, chickens, and other animals that had won their respective county fair categories and earned the right to be shown at the state fair. Photographers exhibited their award-winning pictures. Various stages held live music or other entertainment throughout the day. At night, the large grandstand brought appreciative crowds to see and hear Hollywood stars, country singers, and rock bands. Even horse sulky races sped around the large dirt track at the grandstand. The carnival area contained more rides than any child could possibly survive in one day.

Special food treats never available the rest of the year lured youngsters: saltwater taffy, caramel apples, cotton candy, corn dogs, and Reed's ice cream. However, the most famous item to see was the full-sized cow sculpted from 600 pounds of Iowa butter that was exhibited in a refrigerated glass case. It was never eaten, but a child could try to imagine how many pancakes could be buttered with that much spread.

I yearned to enjoy the fair's excitement. I was annually told, however, that I would not be allowed to attend until I reached age fourteen, since that was the age my father had first been permitted to attend.

Dad and Grandpa Lyle left town one August day each year for excitement, and the womenfolk often stayed at home or on the farm. Grandma Mary, understanding my bitter disappointment, made that our annual special event day. The day required great concentration and awesome responsibility from a young girl. For that was the day Grandma and I washed and polished every item in the china hutch.

The hutch was one of Grandma's treasured possessions. With the ramrod straight back of a soldier at attention, the china hutch stood in its place of honor on the north wall of her home's small dining area. The hutch was five feet high, almost three feet wide, and fourteen inches deep. Shaped in a semi-circle, it had two curved glass sides and a flat glass door. Inside were four wooden shelves.

Highlighted against the light-colored room walls, the china hutch was made from dark wood with an interesting grain. Four slender feet with wheels raised the hutch one foot off the floor. The strength of the wood provided a contrast to the opaque delicacy of its glass sides and front.

The left side of the glass door contained a small metal handle. I could only fit two fingers into the handle grip. To release the latch, I depressed a tiny button above the grip. No one, however, opened the china hutch without Grandma's permission.

No children were allowed to play by the hutch. No chair was placed near it. In all the years Grandma had owned the hutch, it had never been scratched.

The annual cleaning of the china hutch and its dishes was a sacred duty. Like a Japanese tea ceremony, certain ritual preparations had to be observed before the hutch could be opened.

Near the hutch stood Grandma's rectangular dining room table. Only used for Sunday dinners and other special occasions, the table was in pristine condition.

First, I raised the folded leaves to extend the table to full length. Next, the custom-fitted cardboard pads with felt linings covered the table's surface, for the table was never used without them. Over these, I spread a tablecloth and several layers of newspapers, in case of a water spill.

With due solemnity, I carefully carried a white enamel basin of warm dishwater from the kitchen and placed it on the table. Next came an enamel basin of rinse water with a touch of bluing added. Grandma believed the bluing left the dishes with an extra sparkle when they were dried. Finally, I laid dishtowels respectfully beside the basins. Many of those towels had been hand-embroidered by Grandma.

Because of her rheumatoid arthritis, Grandma Mary no longer trusted her hands to lift any delicate object without the fear of dropping it. Thus, on each August cleaning day, she oversaw the ritual, but my hands carried out the duties.

When all preparations were complete, Grandma gave the signal. With trepidation, I opened the glass door. No girlish silliness occurred during those afternoons. Deep concentration was required as I carefully lifted out each item, one at a time.

The china hutch contained the most marvelously delicate objects. A hand-painted china cup and saucer with a floral pattern had been made in England. Beside those rested a set of opaque green-colored glass dessert plates, with matching glasses that had sides so thin I knew they would easily break if I squeezed them.

Next came small, curved, white china plates on which people had placed bones during past meals. Serving platters and bowls, gravy boats, toothpick holders, and decorative cake plates filled the shelves.

The china hutch encased the dreams of over a hundred years of women in my family. Some pieces had been wedding gifts to brides. Others had been inherited at the death of a mother or grandmother. All were revered enough to have endured until now, to be carried in my trembling hands to the table.

As with so many families, the actual history of each piece had never been recorded. Time alone knew the names of which women owned which pieces. Even so, I could feel familiar hands guiding mine as I lifted each item. Those women were in the room, urging me to be cautious, trying to express the pride they had felt in owning the various pieces.

To me, the china hutch symbolized the lives of the women in my lineage. As long as it existed, their memories lived. The special glass and china objects were proof that those now unseen women had existed. They had hoped, prayed, hugged, kissed, and passed on their wishes for the next generations. Those material objects were their legacy to me, and I was awed by the responsibility to care for them.

At last, each item had been washed, dried, and re-turned to the exact spot from which it had been pulled earlier in the afternoon. Then, I gently closed the glass door and released the tiny button to latch the door shut.

My memories of the women in my family were secure for another year. I could almost feel each woman sigh with relief and quietly depart the room.

THE WRECK

Too many families experience a serious car or other accident that alters ordinary life. Such happened to my family when I was twelve years old.

In early May 1965, Mom had worked hard at school all week teaching her fourth graders. Then she hurried home Friday afternoon, loaded Kay and me and our luggage in the car, and drove the two hours to Barnard to visit her mother.

Dad joined us on Saturday, which he rarely did, preferring to stay in Winterset and rest after his week of on-the-road driving for work. We, thus, had two cars to take back to Winterset when early Sunday evening arrived.

Mom wanted me to ride with Dad to keep him awake on the drive home. Kay was to ride with her. Both cars left the same time, but Dad stopped along the way to talk with friends for an hour.

I just wanted to get home and sleep before school Monday morning. When we finally headed north toward Iowa, I was relieved and ready to go.

At Greenfield, Iowa, we turned east on Highway 92, the nearest paved highway to Winterset. As we topped one hill, flashing emergency lights covered the valley's base. An iron bridge with sides that sloped upward, then leveled off with an open top spanned a small creek. In the middle of the bridge was a tangled wreck of something unidentifiable.

The Iowa Highway Patrol officer directed my father's car to the side of the road. The wreck had the bridge closed for the time being until debris could be cleared to allow traffic to pass on one lane. Luckily, that time of night, almost 9:30, no other cars appeared besides ours.

Suddenly, Dad got a strange look on his face. "Stay in the car," he demanded. He exited and headed for the bridge. I watched through the front windshield as he approached the patrolman.

After a few minutes, he returned to the car. I innocently asked, "Was anybody killed?"

He stared at me, quickly started the car, and made a U-turn. "That was your mother and sister!"

He raced back westward toward Greenfield and the nearest hospital. We ran inside and asked where my mother and sister were. The Emergency Room nurse had no idea what we were demanding.

Dad, confused, said, "They couldn't have gone to Winterset, could they?" Then we were back in the car and heading east again. At the bridge, the north lane had been brushed clear of debris so our car could pass. Mother had bought the aqua blue used car about four years earlier, finally having her own transportation when my father was out of town. I looked out my window at the mangled remains of the car, now laying on its roof and mashed almost beyond recognition.

Madison County Memorial Hospital had been serving the needs of local residents for many years. At the Emergency Room, my father found that, indeed, Mom and Kay had arrived and were being treated. Soon eight-year-old Kay appeared, sleepy and terrified after what she had experienced in the last few hours. She still clutched her brown teddy bear in her small arms.

When I approached her, I could see a little blood on

the teddy bear. I took her hand and said, "Let's wash your teddy bear." We headed for the bathroom, where I gently washed out the small spots of blood, trying not to alarm her. We dried the bear with paper towels, then returned to the waiting room.

Mom's injuries were not life-threatening, fortunately. She had fallen asleep at the wheel, with Kay lying across the front passenger seat. When the car began sliding up the bridge railing, Kay had awakened and had asked Mom what was happening. Mom had answered, "We're having a car wreck." Then the car had landed on its roof and spun 180 degrees in the middle of the bridge.

In the days before seat belts, occupants and belongings were tossed around as any crash occurred. Kay had been thrown against the dash and into the back seat, yet was uninjured. Mom's chest had slammed into the steering wheel, her right knee jammed into the dashboard, and her body banged against the door. She would remain in the hospital for many days before coming home to recuperate.

Our home life changed that night, as it had three years earlier when Mom broke her right hip. Unlike that accident, my mother's recovery took longer from the car wreck. She was still on crutches by mid-August, when she was determined to attend the Iowa State Fair. We did go but altered our usual fair sightseeing because she could not walk far.

That night at the State Fair, we had tickets to see the major show at the grandstand. The star was Andy Williams, with the very young Osmond Brothers as the opening act. One gate guard was an old friend from Macksburg who recognized our family. He let us in early to the general admission benches in front of the stage. We enjoyed sitting on the second row to watch the evening's performance.

Such a summer event was our attempt at normalcy. Again, our lives had changed, but we had survived. Our roles had altered, but we had moved on with our lives.

We children were better able to adapt the second time and care for ourselves, since we were three years older. We had learned that life has its disasters, but they must be faced and handled. We had proven quite resilient, though we would have preferred to have waited many more years to discover that particular trait.

THE LAST KISS

Family dynamics are complicated in the best of times. People who live together 24/7 have to learn patience and how to handle a variety of personalities. Some emotional events, however, can change a key relationship for years to come.

One Sunday when I was about twelve, Mom and I had a serious disagreement. The cause has been lost in the mists of time, as occurs with many family arguments. The episode proved unusual in that we rarely reached the point of true anger at each other. We still had not spoken to each other except in unavoidable instances all afternoon and early evening.

Finally, Dad announced bedtime, so Kay and I proceeded to the bathroom to brush our teeth and change into our pajamas. As I walked across the living room, I headed straight for our bedroom.

"Kiss your mother good night!" demanded my father.

I stared at him in anger and defiance. How dare he command me to kiss someone at whom I was almost furious at the moment? That was something I was not prepared to do.

Walking over to Mom's chair, I pressed my lips to her check. It was not a kiss; it was just two pieces of skin touching each other. Then I turned rebelliously to face my father and stalked off to my bedroom.

That was the last time I kissed my mother for many years. Nor did she ever again ask for a good-night kiss.

Every child has breaking away steps toward eventual adulthood. The bonds between child and parent by their very nature must change if a child is to become a responsible, self-functioning adult. Young birds are shoved out of the nest, because they must learn to fly on their own.

The break between Mom and me occurred too early and too drastically. My preteen pride did not allow me to apologize, even though I knew I had hurt her feelings. My mother's kind heart and lack of understanding about how to handle a headstrong daughter could not bridge the gap. We remained loving in other ways, but we never resolved our feelings about that evening's upset.

Handling angry emotions is one of the keys to a healthy ability as an adult to deal with the varied personalities encountered in life. Not all families have that skill nor know how to reconcile emotional wounds. In the mid-1960s, few families ever considered consulting a counselor. The group members were left to deal with the effects of any arguments by themselves. Often, the resulting nonresolution produced family rifts that lasted for years.

Somewhere in my late college years, I was home for a weekend. I felt a true urge to kiss Mom good night, and I did so. No words were exchanged about why it had been so long between kisses. We just smiled, said good night, and parted for our bedrooms.

The long-standing hurt had not been erased, but we had created a bond again between daughter and mother that had been torn apart so many years earlier. From then onward, we both felt more at ease to hug or kiss again. The closer connection felt wonderful.

Made in the USA
Monee, IL
27 August 2021